SIX WEEKS
IN THE
SIOUX TEPEES

Dakota prison camp at Fort Snelling, November 13, 1862. Photo, B. F. Upton, Minnesota Historical Society [E91.45].

SIX WEEKS IN THE SIOUX TEPEES

A Narrative of Indian Captivity

By Sarah F. Wakefield

Edited, Annotated, and with an Introduction by
June Namias

University of Oklahoma Press : Norman

Also written or edited by June Namias:

(ed.) *First Generation: In the Words of Twentieth-Century American Immigrants*, rev. ed. (Urbana, 1992)

White Captives: Gender and Ethnicity on the American Frontier, 1607–1862 (Chapel Hill, 1993)

(ed.) James E. Seaver, *A Narrative of the Life of Mrs. Mary Jemison* (Norman, 1992)

Library of Congress Cataloging-in-Publication Data

Wakefield, Sarah F.
    Six weeks in the Sioux tepees : a narrative of Indian captivity / by Sarah
F. Wakefield ; edited, annotated, and with an introduction by June Namias.
        p.   cm.
    Originally published: Shakopee, Minn. : Argus Books and Job Printing
Office, 1864.
    Includes bibliographical references and index.
    ISBN 0-8061-2975-1 (cloth)
    ISBN 0-8061-3431-3 (paper)
    1. Wakefield, Sarah F. 2. Dakota Indians—History. 3. Dakota Indi-
ans—Wars, 1862–1865. 4. Indian captivities—Minnesota. 5. Minnesota—
Biography. I. Namias, June. II. Title.
    E83.86.W35   1997
    977.6'0049752—dc21   97-2380
                                                                                    CIP

Text is typeset in Scotch.

The paper in this book meets the guidelines for permanence and durability of the Committee on Production Guidelines for Book Longevity of the Council on Library Resources, Inc. ∞

2   3   4   5   6   7   8   9   10

CONTENTS

ILLUSTRATIONS

EDITOR'S ACKNOWLEDGMENTS

WHEN Angelina Grimké protested against slavery she asserted her own freedom: "[T]o be free is to act, to open one's lips in noise and in hope; that free women speak out in public." It is only 150 years ago that women entered into the public forum to speak and write on the issues of politics, race, the family, and their own lot. Like the first women who spoke out on slavery, when Sarah Wakefield spoke and wrote on the issues of war, peace, and the rights of Native people on their own land she was not only disparaged, she was taking on most of the citizens of her state, including—a most difficult position for a woman of her time—her white American and immigrant neighbors who had been through a most fearsome war. I have written earlier of Wakefield's writing and actions as a work of conscience. Here I present Wakefield's text with a considerable introduction and annotations to help place it in ethnographic, historical, and literary context and to raise further moral questions.

I would like to thank the University of Alaska Anchorage, especially its faculty and Dean Wayne C. Miller and the Faculty Development Research and Travel Grants that provided me with time, funds, and research assistants for this project. Kelly Roscoe and Debby LaFleiche helped read through the original text and made suggestions for ways in which I might help both the general and the more scholarly reader with annotations and a clear and accurate text.

My earlier research on the Dakota War was encouraged by John Demos and generously supported by Brandeis University's Department of History and an Irving and Rose Crown Fellowship. The resulting work on Wakefield in *White Captives: Gender and Ethnicity on the American Frontier* was aided by the comments of Laurel Thatcher Ulrich and Neal Salisbury.

I would also like to express my gratitude to Wheaton College and Marilyn Todesco for her work with the Wakefield text. She typed the full 1864 edition onto diskette, thus providing me with a readable, workable, and portable document.

Some of the material in this introduction was presented in earlier drafts and at conferences. The work on motherhood was presented more extensively as "Race, Rape, and Motherhood: Reading Sarah Wakefield Reading the Dakota War" at the American Studies Association annual meeting in Boston in November 1994. I would like to thank Elizabeth Pleck, Paula M. Krebs, and Robin Wallace Kilson for their comments on that paper. "Women as a Moral Force: Indian-White Relations in the Dakota War of 1862" was presented at the annual meeting of the Society for Historians of the Early American Republic, at Boston College, Chestnut Hill, Massachusettes, July 1994. I would like to thank Julie Roy Jeffrey, Susan M. Juster, and the audience for their comments.

Drafts of the introduction were read and commented upon by Herbert T. Hoover, Alan R. Woolworth, Elizabeth Pleck, Daniel Asher Cohen, and Kelly Roscoe. Raymond DeMallie and other reviewers read the material for the University of Oklahoma Press. Alan Woolworth was most gracious in providing me with the identification of several people and places mentioned in narrative. Thanks to Larry Blum and James Jacób Liszka for direction in my foray into moral philosophy. Though they did not read this manuscript, Neal Salisbury, Elise Marianstras, and Calvin Martin deserve thanks for encouraging my continuing work in Indian-white relations. All readers pointed out ways the manuscript could be improved. Any problems remaining are my responsibility.

Papers of the American Board of Commissioners for Foreign Missions are used by permission of the Houghton Library, Harvard University, Cambridge, Massachusettes, and the United Church Board for World Ministries. James Orin Wakefield II gave permission to use Sarah Wakefield's photo.

The Minnesota Historical Society; the Scott County (Minnesota) Records Office; the Tozzer, Schlesinger, Houghton, Widener, and Hilles Libraries—all part of the Harvard University Libraries; the Jacob A. and Bertha Goldfarb Library at Brandeis University; and the Beinecke Library's Western Americana Collection at Yale University provided the sources for my research. The Consortium Library at the University of Alaska Anchorage was a great help as well. I would especially like to thank Sylvia Fink for providing help with interlibrary loan and bibliographic materials.

In Cambridge and in the Boston area I would especially like to thank Natasha Anisimov, Dotty Gonson, Pauline Maier, Adria Steinberg, Patricia Palmieri, Elizabeth MacMahon-Herrera, Sonia Dettmann, Joan Brigham, and Laura Palmer. It is the texture of these women's lives and the quality of their work, thought, and feeling that have, over the years, given me so much inspiration.

In Alaska I would like to thank my colleagues and friends at UAA and in Anchorage, especially Kenneth O'Reilly, Stephen Haycox, Lisa Rieger, Elizabeth Dennison, Carl Shepro, Ron Spatz, Barbara Bradshaw, and Laurel Tatsuda, all of whom helped make this book possible. Greg Protasel has been my greatest friend; his encouragement has made my life and my work more fruitful in every way.

I thank John Drayton, editor-in-chief at the University of Oklahoma Press, for support on this, my second project with the Press. I would also like to thank Sarah Iselin for her help in both editing the manuscript and shepherding it through the process of publication. Thanks too for Ursula Smith's work on editing this edition and to Carolyn Pirnat for additional proofreading.

Finally, I am grateful to my family, especially my son, Robert Victor Slavin, and my sister, Barbara Meltzer, who continually cheered me on. In February 1995 my father, Foster Namias, died, leaving a life of great accomplishment and dedication. For his efforts helping others see clearly and do the best work possible, he is missed and is remembered with awe and with love. These qualities of his have guided me in the scholarly direction I have taken.

A final personal note: Before I first boarded the plane for Alaska in the spring of 1992 I never dreamed that I, a New England girl-turned-woman, would move from the most eastern point of "civilization" in the United States to the "Last Frontier." By that time I had done a good deal of research on Sarah Wakefield, Chaska, and the Dakota War. Before, during, and after my move I thought Sarah Wakefield's narrative more than worthy of a reading by a wide contemporary audience. Now that I spend much of my life in Alaska I feel more than ever the power of her story and the importance of understanding the need for fairness and reconciliation between Native people and those (like myself) who are recent settlers.

JUNE NAMIAS

Anchorage, Alaska

EDITOR'S INTRODUCTION

EDITOR'S INTRODUCTION

IN the late summer of 1862, during the second year of the Civil War, Mdewakanton and Wahpekute Dakotas attacked the Lower Sioux Agency southwest of St. Paul, Minnesota. In the days following, attacking Dakotas fanned out around the agency, moving south toward New Ulm and northwest up the Minnesota River toward the Upper Sioux Agency. They targeted white farm settlements and captured U.S., immigrant, and some Dakota and mixed-blood men, women, and children. The war lasted for six weeks—from August 18 to September 26. It resulted in the deaths of approximately 500 whites, both military and civilian. An unknown number of Dakotas died as well. Some 269 white and mixed-blood Indian and whites, mostly women and children, were taken captive. After the surrender, a military tribunal was hastily organized at a remote site on the upper Minnesota River named Camp Release. There 392 Dakota men and 1 woman were given rapid military trials without counsel, with few or no witnesses, and without interpreters for the many who spoke little or no English. Three hundred and three men were condemned to be hanged. Their records were requested and reviewed by President Abraham Lincoln, who whittled the list of the condemned to 39. On the day after Christmas in 1862, nearly contemporaneously with the issuing of the Emancipation Proclamation, 38 Dakotas were hanged in the largest mass execution in American history.[1]

Six Weeks in the Sioux Tepees is one woman's account of the Dakota War and the events that caused it. Those events forever transformed her life and the lives of thousands of Dakotas and whites in Minnesota. Indeed, the Dakota War of 1862, variously called the Sioux War, the Santee Sioux Uprising, and the Minnesota Sioux Massacre, was the most important event in the history of the state of Minnesota and one of the signal moments in the history of the Dakota people.

In 1862 Sarah Wakefield, a Minnesota woman in her early thirties, was captured in this revolt, along with her four-year-old son and one-and-a-half-year-old daughter. In 1863, shortly after her release, she wrote her narrative defending Dakota rights to Minnesota lands and attacking both state and federal government policy. Although she had sustained a multitude of physical and psychological abuses at the hands of some Natives, all the while fearing her husband's death and expecting death for herself and her children, this woman, whose hair turned white in the six weeks she was in captivity, testified for a Dakota before a military commission hastily assembled about two hundred miles southwest of St. Paul. She chose to testify in front of this all-white, all-male commission only days after these men and their Minnesota regiments had suffered major losses to their units and among their kin. In her testimony she defended a Mdewakanton Dakota who she claimed had saved her life and the lives of her children. For coming to his defense the men of the regiment accused her of adulterous relations with Chaska, or We-Chank-Wash-ta-don-pee, the Indian in question.

In its time Sarah Wakefield's narrative was not a typical reading of the Dakota War. It was delivered during a period of statewide, if not regional, hysteria resulting from the uprising. When the revolt occurred it sent shock waves not only across Minnesota but through the western territories. Territorial governors sent telegrams to Washington warning of impending copycat outbreaks. Since the Minnesota Indian revolt coincided with the beginning of the second year of the Civil War and the brutal Virginia campaigns, reports of the outbreak became more of a regional than a national story. Even so, it soon received national publicity, with both the *New York Times* and *Harper's Weekly* covering the events.[2]

The process leading from government capture of the Dakotas to their execution unfolded as follows. On November 9, the 303 condemned Dakotas, along with close to 360 Dakota men in chains and about 20 Dakota women and children, were marched by the military through the town of New Ulm en route to a camp just west of Mankato. At New Ulm they were attacked by a crowd of German women whose husbands and sons had been killed and wounded that summer in the battle of New Ulm. Commanding officer Col. H. H. Sibley characterized the women as "Dutch she devils" and "tigresses," "who showered brickbuts [sic] and missiles upon the shackled wretches, seriously injuring some fifteen of the latter, and some of the guards."[3]

In late November, Rev. Stephen Return Riggs wrote to the American Board of Commissions for Foreign Missions in Boston of the "great clamor all over the state" for mass execution. Minnesota newspapers demanded annihilation and extermination. "You will understand," he continued, "that in such circumstances, when every body speaks against the Dakotas, it is hard to stand up for them."[4]

While President Lincoln reviewed the trial transcripts and instructed members of his staff to go through them, men like Bishop Henry B. Whipple and eastern reformers urged protection for the Dakotas. At the same time Minnesota congressmen and the press demanded mass execution. The president evaluated the transcripts and on December 11 sent a message to the U.S. Senate explaining that the nature of the case had "caused a careful examination of the records of the trials to be made." As to those "proved guilty of violating females," he concluded, "Contrary to my expectations, only two of this class were found." His order changed the number to be executed from 303 to 39.[5]

Minnesota politicians were outraged. They charged the president with traitorous behavior. Capitalizing on a hysteria focused around the issue of the alleged rape of white women captives, several congressmen charged the majority of the Dakotas with gang rape. In an open letter to Lincoln, which was entered into the Senate records, and published both nationally and in newspapers around the state, Minnesota Congressmen Morton S. Wilkinson, Cyrus Aldrich, and William Windom wrote of what they called "the Indian barbarities in Minnesota." The letter was printed in the same Senate documents that listed the men accused after Lincoln's investigation. It elaborated on the alleged mass rape of Minnesota's white women. It demanded execution of all those accused of "wholesale robbery, *rape, murder*" and claimed, "They seized and carried into captivity nearly one hundred women and young girls, and in nearly every instance treated them with the most fiendish brutality." Describing the women of Minnesota who were captured, the congressmen went on:

> They were the wives and daughters of our neighbors and friends.
>
> They were intelligent and virtuous women; some of them were wives and mothers, others were young and interesting girls. These savages, to whom you purpose to extend your executive clemency, when the whole country was quiet, and the farmers were busily engaged in gathering their crops, arose with fearful violence, and, traveling from one farmhouse to another, indiscriminately murdered all the men, boys, and little children they came to; and although they sometimes spared the lives of the mothers and daughters, they

did so only to take them into a captivity which was *infinitely worse than death.*

Mr. President, let us relate to you some facts with which we fear you have not heretofore been made acquainted. These Indians, whom (as we understand) you propose to pardon and set free, have murdered in cold blood nearly or quite one thousand of our people, ravaged our frontier for a distance of more than a hundred and fifty miles north and south, burned houses of the settlers, and driven from their homes more than ten thousand of our people.[6]

The letter then described "the house of a worthy farmer" whose farm was descended upon by twelve Indians. While the man and his two sons were stacking wheat, all three were shot. The house was entered and two small children were killed and "the sick mother and a beautiful little daughter, thirteen years of age," were both taken captive. After moving the captives to another location, "these fiends incarnate" guarded the sick mother and took the girl "outside of the lodge, removed all her clothes, and fastened her upon her back on the ground. . . . One by one they violated her person" until "they left her dead on the ground . . . within a few feet of a *sick and dying mother.*"[7]

The letter goes on to claim that "a girl of eighteen years of age," known to the congressmen "before and at the time of her capture" as a girl "as refined and beautiful . . . as we had in the State," was taken, bound and tied, and "ravished by some eight or ten of these convicts before the cords were loosed from her limbs. . . . Without being more specific we will state that all or nearly all the women who were captured were violated in this way."[8]

The letter closed by claiming that "there was no justification or pretext, even, for these brutalities," that Agent Thomas J. Galbraith "has labored faithfully and efficiently for the welfare of these Indians; farms have been given out; missionaries have labored zealously among them for their spiritual welfare; money has been paid; farm land distributed." Nor were the Indians "at war with their murdered victims." Finally, reminding the president that they had "stood firm by you and by your administration," the writers "recorded their *protest against pardon*" and warned of the onset of "mob law" in Minnesota unless a full execution occurred without any pardons.[9]

The Wilkinson, Aldrich, Windom letter was reproduced in newspapers around the state and fueled a growing execution fever. In late December the more than three hundred prisoners were all fastened to the brick floor by chains in their Mankato jail. The week of the scheduled hanging the popular journal *Harper's Weekly* reported the story of

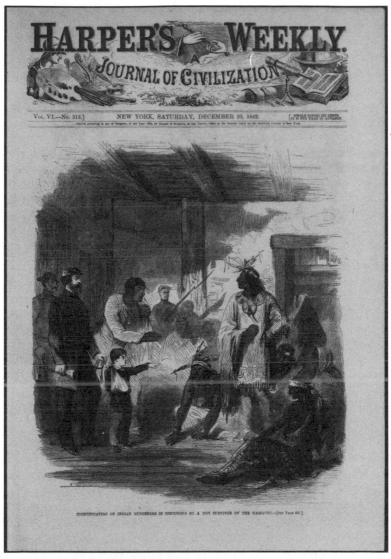

"Identification of Indian Murderers in Minnesota by a Boy Survivor of the Massacre." Cover of *Harper's Weekly*, December 20, 1862. Courtesy of the Widener Library, Harvard University.

a boy who "escaped after seeing the murder and outrage of his mother and sisters." The child was portrayed on the cover of the magazine pointing his finger accusingly at a grotesquely drawn Indian. Thus the reports and the rhetoric of rape helped to create the climate for a mass hanging. The hanging itself became a regional attraction for Mankato, drawing spectators from around Minnesota and from surrounding states. When, on December 26, thirty-eight Dakotas were executed, Sarah Wakefield's "protector" was among those hanged.[10]

The war's devastation, the claims of rape, and the calls for extermination created a climate in which the mass hanging was followed by the banishing of all Dakotas from Minnesota. The Dakota exile was a northern variant of the Trail of Tears—the banishment of the Five Civilized Tribes from the Southeast to Oklahoma in the early 1830s. Most of the remaining Dakota prisoners were sent to an army barracks near Davenport, Iowa. In May 1863, the families of these men, mostly women and children and numbering over thirteen hundred people, were shipped on two steamboats from Fort Snelling to a reservation near Crow Creek in Dakota Territory. Another group went by freight car from Hannibal to St. Joseph, Missouri, and then by boat to Crow Creek, a barren land where, between 1863 and 1866, many Indians died of starvation.[11] Dakota and Winnebago lands were then freely expropriated for the benefit of white settlers.

It was after the executions and the exile that Sarah Wakefield, safely reunited in Shakopee with her husband and their two small children, wrote her narrative. In an atmosphere of vengeance she attacked government policy and defended those Dakotas who had protected her. In a state in which the immigrant and native-born white population had sustained mass murder, the burning of farms, and the orphaning of many children, this young mother took an unusual stand. She defended the Minnesota Dakotas' rights to their ancestral lands and argued for a common humanity across racial and cultural boundaries.

Before presenting Sarah Wakefield's account, I feel a more detailed analysis of the historical, ethnographic, literary, biographical, and philosophical background for the story is in order. First, who were and are the Dakotas? What was the life of these people like before the coming of white settlers and how did it change in those years immediately before the uprising? Second, *Six Weeks in the Sioux Tepees* is a captivity narrative, a particular genre having a prescribed style and content. How does the Wakefield narrative participate in or depart from this genre's traditions? How does that narrative tradition frame this work and what is its history in print? Third, who was Sarah Wakefield?

Why did she write this account? Where did she come from before the war, where did she go at its close? Fourth, in her narrative Wakefield invoked the depth of a mother's love in defense of her actions and thanked the maternal caring of Dakota women. How does this theme of a shared world of motherhood color her reading of the war? Fifth, do the frontier events Wakefield described tell us anything about women and war? Specifically, do they tell us anything about women as a moral force in issues involving ethnic conflict and war?

ETHNOHISTORICAL CONTEXT

The Dakota War was the result of a rapidly growing population of land-hungry Americans and Europeans on aboriginal lands. The impact of that influx intensified in the early years of Minnesota statehood.

In Search of the Dakota People

Images we have of the Sioux spring from impressions widely cultivated and projected onto our imaginations from an early age. These are of Indians on horseback with feather headdresses billowing out over the rumps of horses, shouting war whoops and attacking the good guys, the cowboys. Or they are of "noble" Indians reciting supposedly sacred truths in films like *Dances with Wolves*. The popular culture has given us the Sioux, but those are media creations. They are not the Sioux of the present story.

So too, Western culture created the notion of primitive people and primitive society that shapes our views of certain non-European cultures. In the United States and England the idea was fostered of a superior, more "civilized," society that contrasted with a "savage" or "primitive" society.[12]

The actual Dakotas, or Sioux, have had many names and divisions. They have been called Eastern Dakotas, and Santees. At times they have been called by the particular names of their bands from the villages along the Minnesota River. The word "Sioux" is from the Algonquian-speaking Ojibwas and means "foreigner" or "enemy," but also "adder" or "snake." The Ojibwa term was picked up and shortened by the French from Nadouess-iw' to Naduesiu, finally becoming "Sioux." Dakota-speaking peoples of North America come from 181 eastern and western language groups. Dakota and Lakota are linguistic designations, with Dakota-speaking groups being made up of Mdewakantons, Wahpekutes, Sissetons, and Wahpetons. Eastern Dakotas included these four Dakota-speaking groups, the ones most heavily involved in the war of 1862. The other Sioux, primarily from outside Minnesota

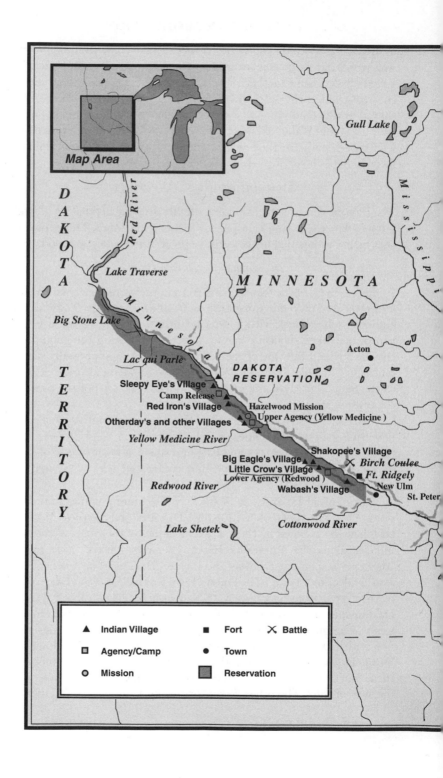

Map Area

Gull Lake

D A K O T A

Red River

Lake Traverse

Mississippi

M I N N E S O T A

Big Stone Lake

Minnesota

Acton

Lac qui Parle

DAKOTA RESERVATION

Sleepy Eye's Village ▲

Camp Release □

Red Iron's Village ▲

Hazelwood Mission

Upper Agency (Yellow Medicine) ▲

Otherday's and other Villages ▲ ◉ □

T E R R I T O R Y

Yellow Medicine River

Shakopee's Village

Big Eagle's Village ▲ ✕ *Birch Coulee*

Little Crow's Village ▲ ▲

Lower Agency (Redwood) □ ■ *Ft. Ridgely*

Redwood River

Wabash's Village New Ulm ●

St. Peter ●

Lake Shetek

Cottonwood River

▲ Indian Village	■ Fort	✕ Battle
□ Agency/Camp	● Town	
◉ Mission	Reservation	

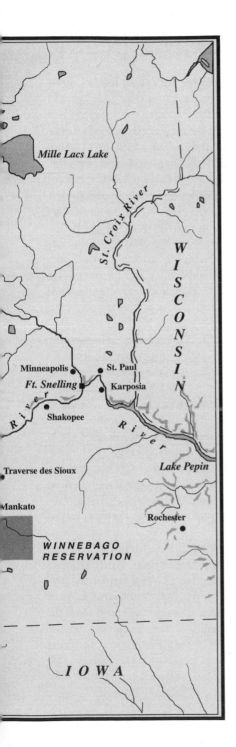

Minnesota in 1862

and living in Dakota Territory or on the high plains at the time of the uprising, included the Yankton, the Yanktonai, and the Lakota-speaking dwellers on the plains.[13]

Numbers are highly contested in Native American history. Estimates before the 1860 Minnesota census were made on the basis of guesses about the number of lodges and the average number of natives per lodge. One scholar, basing his estimate on French records in the upper Mississippi area, suggests "25,000 or more" as a total of all Dakotas in the seventeenth century. Stephen Riggs suggested eight per lodge with "an aggregate Sioux population estimate of about 30,000."[14] Rather than primitive and simple, the Sioux peoples and their relatives were and are complex. Rather than static, feather-wearing, and war-whooping savages, they were diverse, evolving, and difficult to categorize.

The major theme in Dakota history from the coming of the Europeans to the outbreak in 1862 is the growing impact of white incursion. This history is made up of three periods: early European contact (ca. 1600–1787); U.S. territorial years (1787–1858); and early statehood to war (1858–1862).

EARLY EUROPEAN CONTACT: CA. 1600–1787 The French were the first Europeans to come in any numbers to the upper Great Lakes. At the time of their arrival in the 1600s Dakota-speaking people lived near Lake Superior close to the Ojibwas, or Chippewas, an Algonquian-speaking group. The French wanted furs and in exchange for them traded firearms to the Ojibwas, who with their newfound power forced the Dakotas further south. The fur trade and French colonization of the St. Lawrence and Mississippi areas went hand in hand with the missionary impulse. The water route from Montreal and Quebec into the interior was frequently navigated by priests and voyageurs—traveling fur trappers and traders. In the early years, the Dakotas, like the Iroquois but unlike both the Ojibwas and the Hurons, were not interested in converting to Christian ways.[15]

French forts, missions, and settlements spread through the Mississippi Valley in the seventeenth and eighteenth centuries. Kinship bonds developed as first French and then English traders, explorers, and trappers entered the Great Lakes region. In 1766 Jonathan Carver, a British explorer looking for the Northwest Passage, met and lived for half a year with the Sioux. In his journals Carver remarked on the abundance of the Minnesota area and the fact that the Sioux living there were better off than their northern neighbors, the Ojibwas. He also noted the Dakotas' sense of fun and love of dancing and festivities, along with their need to move month to month with their tepees in order to provide adequate subsistence for their families. Dakotas resisted and resented growing French control, predominantly siding with the British in the American Revolution and in the War of 1812.[16]

U.S. TERRITORIAL YEARS, 1787–1858 Following the American Revolution and the Treaty of Paris (1783), the new republic began to assert its claim to the Native land west of the Appalachians then designated as the Northwest Territory. The Northwest Ordinance (1787) claimed the area in Minnesota, Wisconsin, Michigan, Illinois, Indiana, and Ohio for the United States. "The utmost good faith shall always be observed toward the Indians," that act declared, and "their lands and property shall neer be taken from them without their consent." However, land in an eastern corner of Ohio was soon surveyed into townships, and the structures and framework for future settlement were provided, with the stipulations for statehood set in place. The Old Northwest became a major place of settlement for an expanding new nation.[17]

With expanding white settlement, Shawnees, Delawares, and Miamis organized armed protests. But despite early Indian victories, defeat at the battle of Fallen Timbers in 1794 signaled a mass movement of white settlement into the Ohio country. The patterns were set, and by the 1850s the more distant areas of Wisconsin and Minnesota were experiencing even greater amounts of white expansion.[18]

In these early years of the republic, policies of expansion existed side by side with those of paternalism. George Washington's new secretary of war, Henry Knox, favored a policy of accommodation rather than conquest. He proposed to educate and "uplift" Indians with the help of missionaries and advocated restricted use of alcohol. He also called for monitoring trade through a system of government trading houses or "factories" in order to restrict circulation of guns and alcohol and limit the cheating of Indians by white traders. An emerging bureaucratic structure began to take control of Indian lands. Between 1789 and 1795 the Indian Department, under the aegis of the War Department, was designated to administer trade, appoint Indian agents, and establish missions to "civilize" the Indians. Agents were to report back to superintendents and nearby military commanders. This department also supervised the factory system—a far-flung group of government trading posts extending from Detroit on the east to Prairie du Chien on the upper Mississippi and into the southern Mississippi region.[19]

By the early 1800s the four divisions of the Dakotas—Sissetons, Wahpetons, Wahpekutes, and Mdewakantons—still controlled and hunted the lower half of the present state of Minnesota and land on the Wisconsin and Iowa borders. The eight Mdewakanton bands lived close to the Lower Sioux Agency; the Wahpekutes lived as far west as the upper Des Moines. This was a period when French and English traders and trappers met, married, and lived among the Dakotas, but it was also a period when Native people moved more rapidly toward dependency and white control.[20]

After the War of 1812, settlement in the Ohio country proceeded apace. By 1822 factories were discontinued, making individual fur traders, especially those married to Dakota women, an even more important force. In 1824 the Office of Indian Affairs was established by Secretary of War John C. Calhoun to take charge of the disbursal of annuity funds "for the civilization of the Indian." The agency was mandated by Congress to settle and organize Indian affairs.[21]

What happened in the Great Lakes area was related to a wider national policy and political trends taking place in the republic at large. In Minnesota these changes made themselves felt through a series of treaties with Washington. The progression of treaties in the Great Lakes area from the revolutionary period to the years before Minnesota statehood marked the transition from Indian country to white man's land.

According to Gary Clayton Anderson, "the Dakotas had established rewarding and workable relations with Europeans, from whom they benefited in at least two important ways. Traders now regularly carried into Dakota lands goods that enhanced native life." New "metal pots, combs, needles, and knives or other weapons" were "embraced" as they brought a "new material world," even as the meanings of these objects represented different religious and cultural values to the Dakota people. Anderson points out that along with material interchanges "traders became full-fledged members of the Dakota bands, taking wives and fathering children. In the Sioux world view, this obligated them to assist in-laws materially and to help sustain the village."[22] But soon these more equal relationships yielded to a system of diminishing power and dependency.

From the 1820s new federal policy became increasingly tied to notions of the "civilization" of "savages." With land pressures to open Indian country came advocacy of removing "hostile" and "primitive" Natives—even of "noble savages"—in order to "save them from extinction," rather than advocacy of saving them with missions and schools on their home ground. This policy began to dominate relations in Indian country from Andrew Jackson's Removal Act of 1830 until after the Civil War.[23]

According to the Minnesota missionary Samuel Pond, there were about two thousand Mdewakantons in Minnesota in the 1830s. As more missionaries arrived, more treaties were concluded—two at Prairie du Chien (1825 and 1830) and another in Washington (1837). Basically, these treaties were attempts by Washington to clarify and minimize the long-standing disputes between Ojibwas and Dakotas that plagued the Minnesota area and were a nuisance to Indian agents, territorial governors, and the superintendent of Indian affairs.[24] There were also attempts to gain control of Indian land and displace Natives with Anglo-American and European immigrant settlers.

Treaties were the wedge and the badge of legitimacy for white settlement. The Washington treaty (1837) sealed the fate of northwestern Wisconsin lands still under Eastern Dakota claims. A proposal was made that about a million dollars be exchanged for this land, but Mdewakanton leader Little Crow replied, "I see all your people are well dressed—we are obliged to wear skins." He recognized that once the money was divided it would not go far. Other Dakota representatives realized that giving up hunting grounds meant an irreplaceable loss, even though northern Wisconsin's game supply had already been gutted by nearly two centuries of the fur trade. Although the depleted hunting grounds already limited Dakota subsistence and although treaties inevitably led to more white settlement, they were increasingly resorted to by Indians as a means to ameliorate economic disasters and occasional periods of starvation. Treaty provisions promised money for food bought at trading houses, farm tools, and other goods supplied by the "Great Father" (the U.S. government) over a twenty-year period. But in fact, more land for whites meant fewer direct benefits for Natives as special funds were given to traders and the children of ethnically mixed Natives, reducing the initial amounts to be given to the "full-blood" Dakotas. Thus these early treaties created a climate of distrust that clouded the treaties to follow.[25]

In 1849, the year Congress declared Minnesota a territory, the Office of Indian Affairs was moved from the War Department to the Department of the Interior. Commissioners of Indian Affairs became responsible for reservation and land allotment policies. The fate of Minnesota's Indians began to change even more rapidly.

In 1850 Mdewakanton villages still ranged along Minnesota's bountiful waterways from Wabasha's village in the southeast, below

Little Crow, Frank Blackwell Mayer sketch. Photo courtesy of the Edward E. Ayer Collection, the Newberry Library.

Lake Pepin, to Little Crow's at Kaposia south of St. Paul, to Shakopee's central Minnesota village near St. Paul. Territorial status opened up the area in 1850 and 5,000 whites settled in the narrow strip of land between the Mississippi and the St. Crois rivers, an area of rich river land. In the next decade Minnesota's white population shot up from about 6,000 to 172,000—almost 28 times the population in 1850. Minnesota River settlements attracted thousands of Germans, Scandinavians,

English, Irish, and northeasterners who moved into counties south and west of what were to become the Twin Cities.[26]

Population pressures merged with political and economic desires as a new governor, Alexander Ramsey (Whig), and territorial delegate Henry H. Sibley (Democrat), a fur trader and entrepreneur who would play a central role in the Dakota War a decade later, pushed the secretary of the interior to introduce yet another treaty.[27] At Traverse des Sioux on July 23, 1851, Wahpeton and Sisseton Dakotas signed a treaty that exchanged land in the western and southern portions of Minnesota for $1,665,000 in the form of annuities (annual and semiannual payments) and cash. Then on August 5 the Mdewakanton and Wahpekute (Santees) signed a similar treaty at Mendota, giving up lands in the southeastern part of Minnesota for $1,410,000, to be paid over a period of fifty years in annuities and cash. Thus almost 24 million acres of Indian land was opened to settlement in the early 1850s. In exchange, some six thousand or seven thousand Dakotas were placed on two reservations, twenty miles wide and about seventy miles long.

The treaties of Traverse des Sioux and Mendota thus forced Minnesota's Dakotas onto reservation lands located for ten miles on either side of the Minnesota River. This restriction to a narrow strip of river land was a severe blow to their subsistence traditions. As Dakota lands decreased, white population and settlement rapidly increased. The results of the treaties of 1851 brought pressures that were, in effect, the seeds of the uprising of 1862.

The policy of removing Dakotas onto reservation lands was combined with plans to divide that land into farm lots.[28] Between 1853 and 1855 Dakotas moved onto their restricted but still extensive reservation along the Minnesota River. The Upper and the Lower Sioux Agencies had an assigned agent and missions nearby. In 1857 Joseph R. Brown was appointed by the Democrats as agent. His long experience in Minnesota and his marriage to a woman of Dakota origin indicated a knowledge of the area. But Brown strongly believed in the notion of "civilization," opposed the subsistence way of life, and supported the idea of an agricultural allotment policy to improve the life of Natives.

Open conflict between the new white settlers and the Dakotas first came in March 1857. Inkpaduta, the leader of a band of exiled Wahpekutes, attacked a settlement of whites who were squatting on Indian land. The attack was prompted by long-standing irritants. Some of the settlers had stolen horses and sold whiskey, and three years earlier a white man named Henry Lott had "axed to death Sintomniduta and nine women and children." After an attempt of white set-

Treaty at Traverse des Sioux (1851), Frank Blackwell Mayer sketch. Photo
courtesy of the Edward E. Ayer Collection, the Newberry Library.

tlers to disarm the band, Inkpaduta led a counterattack. Thirty
whites were killed near Lake Okoboji in northwestern Iowa, as were
perhaps twelve more across the border in Minnesota. This Spirit Lake
massacre struck fear in the hearts of new white settlers. A militia from
several Minnesota towns was raised, but they were never able to capture Inkpaduta's band.[29]

On June 19, 1858, yet another treaty signed in Washington de-
prived Dakotas of their ten-mile strip of land north of the Minnesota
River and restricted them to a reservation running ten miles wide to
the south of the river. The United States government also claimed the
right to establish any "military posts, agencies, schools, mills, shops,
roads, and agricultural or mechanical improvements" it "deemed necessary." It held the bands responsible for any "depredations" to the extent they could be charged to pay "full compensation" out of annuity
monies owed by the government. Further monies could be withheld if
individuals drank. If members were intoxicated or even bought liquor

for others, the band could lose money "for the period of at least one year" at "the discretion of the secretary of the Interior." As Agent Thomas J. Galbraith wrote in his report of 1863, the idea was "to break up the community system among the Sioux; weaken and destroy their tribal relations; individualize them by giving each a separate home . . . in short *'make white men of them.'"*[30]

A sense of betrayal set in among many young Dakota men. The loss of their lifeways and hunting grounds and the large and continual influx of whites from Europe and the East created a sense of defeat, cynicism, and anger, all of which served as a backdrop to the war. Dakotas who remained true to their traditions, could not be sure their families would not starve. Dakotas who had converted to Christianity and become farmers—"cut hairs"—were favored by new policies, given more money, and were better able to feed their families.

Thus the fate of the Dakotas and their lands was shaped in the years between the crafting of the U.S. Constitution and Minnesota statehood by both local and federal relationships. Millions of acres of Indian land were now opened for white settlement. The government backed a "civilized" agricultural life based on the Jeffersonian presumption that free or yeoman farmers would build a democratic republic. In place of their lands and independence Indians were given reservations and semiannual welfare payments.

EARLY STATEHOOD TO WAR: 1858–62 Statehood came in May of 1858. In 1861, under the new Republican administration of Abraham Lincoln, Joseph R. Brown was replaced as the Dakota agent. With the appointment of Clark W. Thompson as the superintendent of Indian Affairs in the spring of 1862, Thomas J. Galbraith was named the new agent in Minnesota, and a complete reshuffling of reservation workers occurred. Few of these new appointees had the experience or knowledge of the earlier contingent, most of whom had lived in the Minnesota area from territorial days and many of whom had married Dakota women.[31]

With the election of Lincoln also came secession and war. Minnesota, now a new, strongly Republican state, gave its full support to suppressing the Southern rebellion. The call for troops was announced in every newspaper across the state, and the response was overwhelming. Regiments of Minnesota volunteers left for Virginia in June of 1861, fighting and dying at Bull Run in July.[32]

In 1862 there were close to four thousand Dakotas in Minnesota; of these approximately two thousand were Mdewakantons.[33] Little Crow

(Taoyateduta, or His Red Nation), Shakpay, or Shakopee (the elder, also called Little Six), and Wabasha were the leaders of the three most powerful Mdewakanton bands.[34] The bands still took their names from their leaders, but with the new world closing in, traditional ways of life were changing drastically. As spring turned to summer the harvest was poor. Mass starvation became common among the Dakotas as annuity payment time came and no money to buy food arrived at the agencies. Men, women, and children waited in the fields around the Upper Agency, eating unripe fruit from the trees, waiting for food money that should have arrived in late June or early July. At an early August meeting with traders, Dakotas at the Lower Agency pleaded for more food. A trader named Andrew Myrick laughed and told them they could eat grass or even dung. The comment became widely known.[35]

Then, on Sunday, August 17, in Acton, three young Dakotas goaded a fourth to steal an egg from a white farmer. The incident escalated when the Indians called out the farmer, Robinson Jones, ostensibly to join them in target practice and then shot him, his wife, and three guests. The four Dakotas returned to their soldiers' lodge at Rice Creek near Shakopee's village. Indian anger over starvation and overdue annuities was only increased by the realization that such payments would not be given unless the young men were turned in to authorities (as stipulated in the treaties). Very early the next morning, August 18, over a hundred warriors from the Rice Creek and Shakopee villages came downriver to the camp of Little Crow. There they challenged him to confront and avenge the indignities suffered by his people. Lodges of the Mdewakanton were hastily brought together. Division and dissension were rife. Younger men wanted to fight, while many, including Little Crow, thought war would be folly. Despite the division, a fatal decision was reached.[36]

Later, on that same sunny Monday morning of August 18, 1862, the Mdewakantons from Little Crow's village struck the Lower Agency, targeting the stores and those who worked there, whether white, Indian, or mixed blood. Several men were killed, barns were seized, guns and supplies were taken. The Dakotas fanned out around the agency with plans to attack white settlements along the Minnesota River. The war was on.[37]

The Dakota World

Before, during, and after the war, much of the Dakota world was shrouded from foreigners. Yet to understand Dakota ways of kinship, spirit, ceremony, thought, and daily life is to have some awareness of the world behind the uprising. Although far from discernible by Sarah

Wakefield, Dakota ways were central to her life in Minnesota. Indeed, religion and kin relations were oftentimes misinterpreted by her and other white settlers. One such early example was the missionary Samuel Pond's description of Dakota beliefs and ceremonies as "chaotic fragments" and "superstitions" prompting "idolatrous" behavior.[38]

There is little direct information about traditional spiritual life from nineteenth-century Dakotas themselves. One exception is Charles Alexander Eastman (Ohiyesa) who was four years old at the time of the Dakota War. His grandmother was a Mdewakanton who married the artist Seth Eastman. Ohiyesa remembers how as a boy he and his family left Minnesota for Dakota Territory and Canada after the war. He recounts starvation, prairie fires, blizzards, and near-disastrous river crossings in the summer and fall of 1863, as soldiers chased his family into Dakota Territory. Ultimately he spent much of his early life on a reservation.[39]

Eastman speaks of the Great Mystery, the central creative principle in Sioux life—*wakan*, which by its nature is indefinable. In Western mystical traditions *wakan* might be close to Talmudic notions of the ineffable nature of God. The Oglala Indian Good Seat found the word itself applied when "anyone did something that no one understood." A great mysterious event was Wakan Tanka: "How the world was made is *Wakan Tanka*. How the sun was made in *Wakan Tanka*. How men used men used to talk to the animals and birds was *Wakan Tanka*. Where the spirits and ghosts are is *Wakan Tanka*. How the spirit act is *wakan*. A spirit is *wakan*."[40]

The traditional way to approach a relationship with something *wakan*, was through the sacred pipe, which came to the Sioux people as a gift from White Buffalo Calf Woman. The tobacco used, the holding and filling of the pipe bowl, the way the pipe was passed around the fire were all sacred rituals. Wakefield saw and used tobacco and a pipe, but hardly recognized its sacred functions. Raymond J. DeMallie explains that "in Sioux society kinship provided the driving force of everyday life," and that kinship is linked with the symbols of the culture. "The sacred woman came bearing the gift of the pipe, the foundation of the Sioux way of life," DeMallie notes, and the "pipe itself is the symbol of kinship." Thus the spiritual and the societal are closely linked.[41]

Festivities and ceremonials involving public and secret performance with drums, speeches, chants, and dance marked the calendric rituals of the Dakota year. Samuel Pond found these "were great occasions, often drawing together nearly all the population of two or three villages," with the observers and participants showing "solemnity" and

Group of Dakotas in front of Chaska's house, 1862. Whitney's Gallery, Minnesota Historical Society [E91.7u/ri].

observing "the strictest decorum." Sacred, or *wakan*, feasts were commonly held where men chanted in prayer. Large amounts of food were prepared, and fellowship and relationships among kin were strengthened. To the missionary's eyes, food "was often lavishly expended in these feasts" as a show of generosity to and reciprocity with one's neighbors. Yet this feasting alternated with fasting was a puzzle to Pond and other whites who observed such practices, which were in fact common in the subsistence cultures of the Americas and reflected seasonal abundance and scarcity.[42]

Although the Dakota people rebuffed early missionaries, later ones had better luck. Samuel Pond and his brother Gideon Pond arrived in the territorial period with other evangelizing Protestant ministers. John P. Williamson, his son Thomas S. Williamson, and Stephen Return Riggs represented the American Board of Commissioners for Foreign Missions. Episcopalian Bishop Henry Benjamin Whipple worked with Ojibwas. Catholics, too, successfully proselytized among the indigenous peoples in the Great Lakes region. By the 1850s and early 1860s churchmen had powerful constituencies among both the Dakota people and those of mixed Indian and white heritage. "Christian Indians" were commonplace and identifiable. They were called "cut hairs," because the men cut their long hair short, wore white men's clothes, lived in cabins, and farmed. They were living symbols of white inroads into Indian country. With the churchmen came the closing of traditional lands and limits on hunting. Common festivals were eliminated or reduced in number. Christianity brought individualism, revising the ways of the sacred, of reciprocity and generosity, and of gender roles. Men were urged to farm rather than hunt. Girls formerly taught the values of generosity, bravery, patience, and wisdom were taught instead to sew and to aspire to the norms of True Womanhood.[43]

Generally, those Dakotas closer to white settlement were more acculturated, coming as they did under some Christian influence. Even so, they still practiced Dakota rituals and adhered to Dakota beliefs. Chaska, Wakefield's "protector," was a man in the middle: born into a traditional Dakota world, he had begun to move into the new world of accommodation. But his treatment and his mother's treatment of the Wakefield family appears traditional. According to DeMallie, Sioux kin were defined not only as blood relations but as those who shared the ways of the people. These included captive women "from other tribes . . . when they learned to speak the language and act according to Sioux ways." Captured children too "were not distinguished in any way from other Sioux children." These actions were part of cultural and social practice that included adoption where "the heart of the kinship system" was a contract with Wakan Tanka uniting "all forms of being into an unbroken network of relationship" and creating "kinship as the foundation of morality."[44]

It is likely that Wakefield was seen as kin by many of the Dakota people during her captivity, and her children were protected as if they were Dakota children. Although the world of accommodation and forced acculturation came abruptly to the Dakotas, among many Dakota people the spirit world and sense of kinship remained strong. Spirit was everywhere and the old ways persisted with the new among these people of the lakes and prairies of Minnesota.[45]

CAPTIVITY NARRATIVES AND SARAH WAKEFIELD'S NARRATIVE

In *Six Weeks in the Sioux Tepees* Sarah Wakefield offers us an entree into the Dakota world and the world of Indian-white conflict through a well-established American genre. No set of writings brought the worlds of white American settlers on successive American frontiers more immediately before the nineteenth-century public than the reports of Indian capture. The words and images of these experiences were printed in local papers, in pamphlets, and in books of the day. Captivity narratives were widely published and republished on both sides of the Atlantic. Narratives recounted the trials, survival, and sometimes loss—either to Native societies or to death—of fathers and sons, mothers and daughters. Narratives of captivity were the first original American literary genre; they were also the first writing of any length by or about American women.

Until recently, captivity narratives were seen by scholars primarily as propaganda used to encourage land grabbing and the displacement of the Indian. Roy Harvey Pearce first noted the change in the genre from its inception as a form of Puritan religious writing like the narrative of Mrs. Mary Rowlandson (1682) to a more sensational and sentimental genre in the nineteenth century, when the tales often became "wild and woolly." Richard Slotkin found them master narratives that created a mythic conception of the frontier, justifying violence as a way to regenerate American society. Today, we recognize different ways of reading the narratives. My earlier work, *White Captives*, discusses an alternative narrative tradition, which includes James E. Seaver's *A Narrative of the Life of Mrs. Mary Jemison* (1824) and John Dunn Hunter's *Memoirs of a Captivity among the Indians of North America* (1824), both of which display more sympathetic and detailed accounts of native life. Although not the story of long-time captivity like those other two works, Wakefield's is also an alternative narrative. At a time when the state and national press were calling for extermination of the Dakotas or their forcible deportation from Minnesota, she attacked government policy and defended many Dakotas.[46]

But why bother bringing another captivity narrative to the attention of the modern reader? Haven't we had enough stories and films of violence? If the events of Wakefield's narrative are not widely known outside of the Minnesota region, why revive this history?

First, Wakefield's narrative offers useful clues to the ethnographic record of that strange breed of Euro-American man and woman who headed West in the nineteenth century. It documents notions of family, religion, race, propriety, cleanliness, sexuality, and gender roles along with the actual responses of whites and Indians and the responses presumed appropriate or inappropriate during times of war or rebellion. Historians of early America have fewer resources than those chronicling the twentieth century, so primary documents from men and women who moved west or who lived on the borders between white and Indian worlds are useful, however tentative the evidence.

Second, Minnesota was home to thousands of new immigrants and many families of mixed Native and French or Native and Anglo-American heritage. Of course, in using such narratives to assess people and events, the scholar, the student, and the general reader have to go slowly.

Finally, more than a decade ago Neal Salisbury pointed out the rather one-sided viewing captivity narratives received from the scholarly community. With few exceptions, approach to the narratives as myth and literature dominated discussion, and the works were seen only as creations of the white imagination—as propaganda rather than as potential historical or ethnographic sources. Salisbury argued that although this literature was a cultural phenomenon that drew Indians in "moral and psychological abstractions," it was more. These accounts offer valuable information on Amerindian warfare, he claimed, its "rituals, tactics, movements, leadership, the treatment of prisoners, the conditions of non-combatant life, and diplomacy."[47] A careful reading of Wakefield's narrative uncovers all of these things and documents the impact of white expansion and Dakota resistance in the new West.

THE WRITER AND HER WRITING

It is hard to assess the mythic and fictional realms while trying to extricate ethnographic and historical material, but Wakefield's narrative has much to offer historians and ethnographers, as well as students of literature, gender, and moral philosophy. Before we proceed through her captivity narrative, we want to know more about the writer and her work.

Just who was Sarah Wakefield? She was born Sarah Brown on September 29, 1829, in Kingston (or Kingstown), Rhode Island, the daughter William Brown and Sarah [?] of North Kingston.[48] Why, when, and how she came to Minnesota is uncertain, but after she moved there the record becomes more clear.

Her husband, John Luman Wakefield, is easier to trace. He was born on May 25, 1823, into a politically active family from Winsted in Litchfield County, Connecticut. He graduated from Yale Medical School in 1847. His younger brother James Beach (b. 1828) was educated at Trinity College in Connecticut and became a lawyer. The Wakefield brothers moved west to Minnesota and settled in Shakopee, where James became a successful land speculator, a state and then a federal legislator. John set up a medical practice in Shakopee and married Sarah Brown (listed in the Scott County marriage records as Sarah Butts) on September 27, 1856. He was listed as thirty-three years old, she as twenty-eight.[49]

In 1860 the Minnesota census for Scott County listed John L.

Wakefield as a thirty-seven-year-old physician, with a wife Sarah of thirty-one years, and a child, James O[rin], born in Minnesota and then three years old. Dr. Wakefield's personal estate was valued at $500 with no real estate. Ten years later the Shakopee city directory listed the doctor as forty-seven years old and his wife as forty years old. His personal estate was valued at $1,000 and his real estate at $4,500. By the time of the 1862 uprising, Sarah's second child, Lucy E. (Nellie) was about one and a half years old. In the years following the uprising Sarah had two additional children. Thus in the 1870 census she was shown to be the mother of four children: James Orin, twelve years old; Lucy, ten; Julia E., four; and John R., two.[50]

At the outset of the Dakota War, Sarah Wakefield was a tall woman, thirty-three years of age, with light brown hair (during her captivity she would turn thirty-four). She weighed close to two hundred pounds. From her own descriptions, photographs, family records, and legal claims we can reconstruct the following: although she had moved onto the Minnesota frontier, she retained a taste for eastern fashion. She followed contemporary trends in both clothing and culture, having subscriptions to *Godey's, Harper's Weekly, Peterson's, Eclectic*, and *Mothers'* magazines. Her wardrobe included silk, cashmere, linen, and chenille dresses and even a green velvet hat with feathers. For cold weather she had kid and beaver gloves, an otter muff and cuffs.[51]

If we presume that in a family such as theirs John Wakefield provided the income, we can also assume that Sarah used it to decorate and shape the household. We find her a woman interested in constructing as comfortable a home as can be imagined on a frontier as remote from a city parlor as the Upper Sioux Agency. The Wakefields' house was next to the agent's quarters and warehouse building. It contained five rooms: a parlor, "family room" (or bedroom), dining room, kitchen, and "help's room." The Wakefield parlor included a walnut table, a rocker, a sewing chair, a cabinet, a mahogany side table, a green damask sofa, pictures, miniatures, vases, and bound books. The family room too was full of mahogany furniture and carpets. The dining room had two bird cages, each housing three canaries. Reflecting a properly Christian and educated household, there were also a family Bible and a hymnbook, along with songbooks, a grammar, a geography, and other books and maps.[52]

Besides enjoying a comfortable home, Sarah Wakefield was used to presiding over elaborate meals with a great array of dishes and glasses. Even at the Upper Agency the Wakefields' five-room home had a fully equipped midnineteenth-century kitchen including six- and ten-quart porcelain pots; all manner of glass goblets, egg glasses, and tumblers; breakfast, dinner, and tea plates; tureens and ladles; platters; a carving set; a fifteen-quart brass tea kettle and sixteen-quart coffee kettle; and a variety of damask towels, napkins, and tablecloths.[53]

The Wakefield family possessed a fully stocked larder with pounds of coffee, brown and green tea, pork, dried beef, ham, codfish, mackerel, cheese, crackers, sardines, rice, butter, lard, eggs, sugar (crushed, brown, and powdered), flour (regular and buckwheat), cornmeal, spices, and one or two seasons' worth of preserves. In the summer of 1862, a summer when food was scarce for Dakota families in Minnesota, the Wakefields claimed to have one hundred pounds of pork, seventy-five pounds of dried beef, one hundred fifty pounds of ham, fifty pounds of codfish, one keg of mackerel, forty-five pounds of cheese, fifty pounds of crackers, seventy-five pounds of rice, one hundred pounds of butter, and ten dozen eggs. Even half of that would have been a substantial store. In addition, at the time of the outbreak, the Wakefields owned chickens, including thirty-nine hens, a cow, and a pig.[54]

In short, Sarah Wakefield was the wife of a young and prospering doctor. If not living as comfortably as someone of her station would in New York or Philadelphia, in the new West she was a woman from a family of some means. Of course, she had an Indian woman for "help." In the East, or even in midwestern cities, a woman of her position might have had several maids.[55] She mentions only one. How the work was divided and what if any housework her husband did, we do not know.

Finally, the Wakefields owned a mare with a harness. Although Sarah Wakefield neither tells us of her specific taste in foods nor discusses home decorations, she clearly states her joy for horseback riding. Her descriptions of her rides around the agency area and the river nearby tell us something of the freedom she felt as a woman on horseback. So, too, her writing about the Dakota women she met while on those somewhat-forbidden rides gives us a sense of a woman ready to explore not only her physical surroundings but her cultural surroundings as well.[56]

The decade between 1860 and 1870 was the critical one for Sarah Wakefield and her family. From a privileged life they moved into a threatened existence. At the end of her captivity in 1862 Sarah Wakefield made a fateful decision: to go before the military commission and defend a man she called Chaska. In Case No. 3, We-Chank-Wash-ta-don-pee, Sarah Wakefield testified in defense of the man she named as her "protector." In the first half of her testimony, she tried to clear him of the murder of George Gleason, a man hired by her husband to drive her and their children to safety. In the second half she testified that he had "prevented" another Indian from killing her. He "saved my life once," she said, "when Shakopee, the chief of his band tried to kill me." She testified too that Chaska was "a very generous man," giving away "his own shirt" to other Indians.[57]

In the years following the war and Wakefield's brief notoriety as a writer, the fortunes of her husband, John Wakefield, fell. On February 17, 1874, the fifty-year-old doctor was found dead in his home, most likely of an overdose of drugs. Whether these were administered by accident or deliberately is hard to determine. Dr. Wakefield appears to have been a drinker with a taste for many consumer goods—more than he could afford. From an estate valued at over $5,500 his wife was left, after paying his bills, with only a couple of thousand dollars. Debts claimed the lion's share of the doctor's land and income. Two years after his death, his widow and and four children moved to the outskirts of St. Paul.

Sarah Wakefield spent the final twenty-three years of her life in St. Paul. She died on May 27, 1899, at the age of sixty-nine. Two days later, the *Saint Paul Pioneer Press* wrote a five-paragraph story under the headline: "Death of Mrs. Wakefield, In Minnesota Since 1854. She was a Prisoner of the Sioux for Six Weeks During Their Outbreak."[58]

Six Weeks in the Sioux Tepees: A Narrative of Indian Captivity first appeared in print within a year after the release of Sarah Wakefield and her children. Why did Wakefield put pen to paper in the first place and why and how, once the book was published, did she alter her story?

As to the first question there are at least six answers. In the preface to both editions Sarah Wakefield tells the reader that the work was not intended for public consumption but rather as a record for her children. Fair enough. But she continues: "I do not pretend to be a book-writer" and goes on to warn the reader not to expect "much to please the mind's fancy." Apologies and disclaimers aside, Wakefield was first of all a writer. She wrote with a flare. She expanded her second edition in 1864 because she recognized her talent and gained confidence in her ability to create powerful scenes of human drama. In the second edition she persuasively sets up her story, tracing in the setting, the backdrop of that first night of fright, the July Fourth incident, and the habits of the traders.[59]

In the second edition, she also expands her introductory material by nine pages in order to develop her major theme: the mistreatment of the Dakotas, which she saw as at the heart of the tragedies that were

Sarah F. Wakefield, date unknown. Courtesy of *St. Paul Pioneer Press* and James Orin Wakefield II.

to follow. She describes the background of the war by telling the reader how in August of 1862 the Dakotas came in for their annuities and "camped out" a mile from the agency buildings. "Here they remained many weeks, suffering from hunger—every day expecting their pay so as to return to their homes."[60] This second edition more fully articulates a pro-Indian story; in the tradition of the alternative captivity narrative, it argues for compassion and understanding. Sarah Wakefield wrote with a moral message.

Besides this need to write and to convey a moral message, Sarah Wakefield had a third motive in publishing the narrative. She wanted to clear her name, both for herself and for her family. Rumors were spread about her. Had she slept with Chaska? Had she become his wife? Did she love him? How could she return to her husband if this was the case?[61]

Fourth, if Wakefield and her family wished to remain in Minnesota, she had to make peace with white Minnesotans, many of whom saw her as a traitor. Other captives claimed that she had sided with the enemy. To some of the white captive women around her, her behavior was judged as too cooperative. Captive Mary Schwandt wrote:

> Mrs. Dr. Wakefield and Mrs. Adams were painted and decorated and dressed in full Indian costume, and seemed proud of it. They were usually in good spirits, laughing and joking, and appeared to enjoy their new life. The rest of us disliked their conduct, and would have but little to do with them. Mrs. Adams was a handsome young woman, talented and educated, but she told me she saw her husband murdered, and that the Indian she was then living with had dashed out her baby's brains before her eyes. And yet she seemed perfectly happy and contented with him![62]

From the first, Wakefield asserts the prime motivation for her behavior: to protect herself and her children. She disguised her boy James by rubbing dirt on him so that he would not appear white to the Indians who she heard were looking to kill him. She tore the dress off little Nellie to expose her darker skin. She even seriously considered killing her baby girl. "What I suffered," she says, "let every mother imagine, when you think of my trying to cut my child's throat myself." Here her tale takes on the classic lament of the early Puritan women's narratives: "I have passed through many trials and different scenes, but never suffered as I did then. God so willed it that a storm arose as the sun went down, and a furious storm it was. . . . Surely God gave me strength, or I would have died through fear for I am by nature a very cowardly woman."[63] Through confessing her female weakness and maternal need to protect her children, she hoped to clear herself of the charges of unpatriotic and irrational actions.

A fifth motive may have been to clear her own conscience. The man who had protected her and her children ultimately gave his life. Had she done enough to save him? Yes, she testified in his behalf. But could she have done more? Did this woman write to expunge her sense of guilt and to erase any sense of shame her family might have had about her? Whether morality or personal guilt directed her efforts, if her writing could not bring Chaska back, it could at least prick the conscience of white Minnesotans who had banished the Dakotas. Toward that end, she expresses sorrow for "my neighbors" who "lived like the white man; now they are wanderers, without home, or even a resting place." Their land along the Minnesota River "was a portion of the most beautiful country that was ever known, and they had everything they wished to make them comfortable if they could have only stayed there." But, Wakefield continues, "a few evil men commenced their murderous work, and all has gone to ruin."[64]

A final motive for writing was clearly to sell her story. Wakefield produced two editions of *Six Weeks in the Sioux Tepees*. In the preface to her first edition she printed "November 25, 1863." The second edition has the same date but was published in 1864. The small pamphlets came in colored paper covers, printed on rough, inexpensive paper. Wakefield's tracts were made to sell fast rather than to endure. The second edition added a frontispiece with a picture of Little Crow. Its back cover asked for agents to sell the book.[65]

How many booklets she sold and how much money she made we do not know. Was the book really only written for her children? Which of these six motives dominated her writing: to be a writer? to convey a moral message? to clear her sexual reputation? to refute charges of treason? to purge herself of guilt? to make a profit? Were there others? Let the reader be the judge.

As to the changes made between the two editions: the second edition was the longer. The 1863 edition had fifty-four pages, while the 1864 edition was expanded to sixty-three pages. This nine-page addition of tiny print would represent closer to eighteen pages in today's larger typefaces. The expansion of the booklet added nearly 18 percent new material to the original. In the enlarged edition, with fifty lines to a page, a total of 653 lines were added. The new material centered around four themes: the mother/survivor role; Chaska and Dakota life; the threatening nature of life in Indian captivity; and issues of conscience. This additional material contributed greater detail and depth to the original story. This fuller story enhanced Wakefield's claim as a moral writer.[66]

MOTHERHOOD AND THE ROLE OF DAKOTA WOMEN

Who was Sarah Wakefield then? She was a woman who believed, like the Dakotas themselves, in the reciprocal nature of human relations.

The hanging at Mankato, December 26, 1862, from *Leslie's Illustrated Newspaper,* January 24, 1863. Engraving by W. H. Childs. Courtesy of the Minnesota Historical Society [E91.45 p. 49].

Chaska and his family helped her; she must help them. She was also a woman who believed in fairness, a woman willing to take risks for others, and a woman with a strong identification as a mother.

Early in 1863, only weeks after Chaska's hanging, Sarah Wakefield composed the first edition of her narrative. In both it and the second edition she amplifies and gives any number of variations on the theme of both Christian and Dakota motherhood. She uses her status as a mother to justify her actions and her feelings and then to go on to defend her "protector," Chaska. After Chaska first saved her on the prairie, he again interceded:

> O, how happy was I! My life was again saved, and by him. Had not God raised me up a protector among the heathen? Have I not reason to bless His name, and thank the man and his family for all their goodness towards me and mine? for my little children would now be motherless if he had not taken care of me.[67]

Besides defending her own actions and setting them in the context of motherhood, besides defending Chaska's actions and describing them as a heroic defense of a mother and children, Wakefield goes on to recognize the role of Dakota mothers in saving her life and the lives of her children.

It was Chaska's mother who first recognized that Wakefield's and her children's best chance to survive was if they were dressed as Dakotas. Wakefield says of the beginnings of her captivity that she was told "to go to [Chaska's] mother's tepee in the morning, and tell her to give me a squaw dress, saying I would be more safe in such an attire."[68]

On Tuesday, September 19, a month into her captivity, as the Mdewakanton Dakotas were preparing to attack Fort Ridgely, Wakefield describes yet another set of disguises contrived by Dakota mothers to protect her. "I went to Chaska's mother, and soon I was changed from a white woman to a squaw." Claiming to feel humiliated in these clothes, she nonetheless allows an old woman to rub "dirt into my skin to make me look more like a squaw." Still later, when her life was threatened, it was Chaska's mother who came to warn her that a man was going to kill her, took up her daughter, Lucy (Nellie), on her back, and had Wakefield take her son, James, to safety. "She gave me a bag of crackers and a cup, and we ran to a ravine. . . . and bidding me sit still, left me saying she would come in the morning." Later Chaska's mother again took charge of her, taking the white woman and her daughter to the woods and telling her to sit in a brook "until sunset" when she would return. "I could not refrain from giving her a good kiss. I learned to look upon that woman as I would upon a mother, and I hope some day to be able to do something for her."[69]

Along with Chaska's mother, another Dakota woman crossed the cultural boundaries and helped Wakefield and her children. This woman went by the appropriate name of Mother Friend. Wakefield writes that when she met "with some of my best friends" in the Shakopee band, "an old squaw called by the whites 'Mother Friend,' was there, and glad was I to see her." Several times she mentions the kindness of this woman who treated her child as her own.[70]

Wakefield convincingly demonstrated the caring and humanity of these two Dakota women toward her and her children during the uprising. Unlike Chaska, who was implicated in Gleason's and other whites' deaths, these women needed no defense. But Wakefield, through her continual discussion of their actions, undermines the cries for extermination and banishment of the Dakotas from the state of Minnesota following the war. She seeks to protect these women, to repay them for their generosity, and to build a coalition based on the bonds of motherhood.

In the days after the white release came the Indian captivity. As

The handwritten order from Pres. Abraham Lincoln to Brig. Gen. H. H. Sibley listing 39 Dakotas to be hanged. Before the hanging at Mankato, one of the condemned men received a reprieve. We-Chank-Wash-ta-don-pee, Case No. 3, "Chaska," was not on the president's list, but Case No. 121 had a similar name, as did others who were among the 392 tried. Courtesy of Minnesota Historical Society Reserve Collection, Edward Duffield Neill Papers (A.N41le), December 6, 1862, Order of President Lincoln.

the military closed in on Chaska and others, despite (and some say because of) Sarah Wakefield's defense, it was Chaska's mother who needed Wakefield. Chaska, along with several hundred other Dakota men, was placed under arrest. Two days before she left Camp Release, Wakefield visited the camp where the Dakotas were held. In her account Wakefield shows the desperation of Chaska's mother, a desperation as real as her own but even more futile.[71] Perhaps she felt as guilty for not helping the mother as she feld for not being able to save the son. Perhaps these guilts forced her to become a writer in defense of the Dakota nation. The nature of mothering, of mothering one's own children but also of caring for those who cared for her, was a powerful force in this woman and in her reading of the Dakota War. It is a theme played out here using some of the conventions of both the captivity narrative and the women's fiction of the day.[72] Through the theme of motherhood Wakefield hoped to evoke in her reader a more sympathetic view of "the enemy."

WOMEN AS A MORAL FORCE

My grandmother witnessed the hanging of her father in Mankato when she was thirteen years old. The families were there to watch. It was a tragedy. . . . But before my grandmother died, she told me about it. She wanted me to know my history. She told me of her grief. And of her fear. . . . From my grandmother I learned about sadness. . . . My grandmother and her family marched along with the prisoners to be with their father when he was executed. The men were stripped of whatever they had—their clothing, their blankets, their peace pipes. . . . Old people and some women and children were left behind in the Minnesota Valley. They stayed all winter in their tipis, hungry and sick. Then in May 1863 they were driven from their homes.[73]

—Rose Bluestone
(Wahpekute Dakota/Mdewakanton Dakota)

Today, as in Sarah Wakefield's time, ethnic and racial rivalries and violence surround us. In these situations, are women more caring and more aware of others? Are they a moral force?[74]

As far back as Aristotle, a woman's moral judgment was accorded inferior status. Aristotle claimed that "the courage of a man is shown by commanding, of a woman in obeying. And this holds in all other virtues."[75] By Wakefield's day philosophers still considered men as morally superior and women as moral lightweights, while society at large viewed middle-class women as beacons of moral superiority. In

Western European and American life the domestic sphere was said to protect "the angel of the house." Besides dispensing grace and charm as mother and wife, a woman was admired for her moral purity. She was above the fray of the marketplace, where men were turned into beasts. Though this popular view stressed middle-class women's moral superiority in terms of attention paid to the care of their own household, women still held an inferior moral and intellectual status. Arthur Schopenhauer considered women's powers to reason weak and offered that this contributed to their ability "to show more sympathy for the unfortunate than men do." On the other hand, weak reasoning ability made them "inferior to men in point of justice, and less honorable and conscientious." The "concrete things which lie directly before their eyes" he found overwhelmed "abstract principles of thought." Thus he found women "far less capable than men of understanding and sticking to universal principles." Even more critical was Immanuel Kant, who found women *incapable* of higher moral principles.[76]

In our own time, an argument regarding the nature of female morality is in the forefront of contemporary moral philosophy and feminist theory and has something to say about the Dakota case. In her book, *In a Different Voice,* Carol Gilligan has presented an argument for women's equal if not superior moral reasoning. Based on, but challenging the earlier work by Lawrence Kohlberg, Gilligan posits a hierarchy of stages in moral reasoning. Kohlberg assumes a "theory of moralization" with six sequential stages of "development of personality," where individuals move from the bottom to the top of a pyramid based on their level of logical reasoning. At the very highest stage is a sense of "personal commitment" to higher standards with a sense that morality is an end in itself.[77]

Gilligan's research finds that, rather than operating on abstract principles of justice, women tend to deal with *concrete* moral decisions grounded in relationships. She calls these means of judging moral issues *different* from but not inferior to the justice model of Kohlberg, thus setting women on an equal plane with men. Her model, however, goes even farther, implying that the "different voice" of women is actually superior to men's. Rather than insisting that a moral proposition must be situated in a higher notion of justice, Gilligan claims women make choices on the basis of "caring." Sara Ruddick, another contemporary moral theorist and feminist critic, claims that "women's moral reasoning yields a morality of love" and that in opposition to warfare and allegedly male aggressive postures, women's ways give us a critique of a militaristic way of thinking.[78]

"Like a Destructive Storm"

If women do have a more caring perspective, why, I wondered, was Sarah Wakefield the only white woman to step forward, from the hundreds of women held captive or otherwise involved in the war, to defend Dakota people?[79]

Looking at the accounts of other women directly involved in the Dakota War, it should be said in their defense that they were hardly moral philosophers by profession. Rather, they were caught in the crossfire of a racial and cultural war for land. Women were amazed by the war's impact upon themselves and their families. Many years later Esther Wakeman (Mahpiyatowin, or Blue Sky Woman) remembered the events of August: "Like a destructive storm, the war struck suddenly and spread rapidly."[80]

Most white women's accounts show that they did see the ethical issues of war. In the Minnesota case, women looked at the moral issues in war from a two-tiered vantage point: one concrete and one abstract. In the concrete, the war created personal *crisis points* in moral relations. When someone has a gun to your head you usually do not make the clearest of philosophical judgments. But although these crisis points usually involved violence or potential violence to loved ones, women had options and moral frames of reference. This *moral vantage point* usually came later, in a state of relative tranquility, after the crisis point had passed. It required the possession of an overview or a moral frame of reference. But for most Minnesota women who wrote about their experiences, the intensity of war and earlier ethnic rivalry brought crisis points that overwhelmed more abstract moral judgment.[81]

CRISIS POINTS   Crisis points were traumatic in the extreme.[82] Minnie Buce Carrigan was a German immigrant child who came with her parents to Wisconsin in 1858 and later moved to Minnesota. Forty-one years after the events she remembered "that dreadful Monday" of August 18, 1862, when a large group of Indians came to her house. As a seven-year-old she watched her father die as a Dakota man leveled a double-barreled shotgun at him and then shot him along with her mother and baby sister.[83]

At twenty-seven, Justina (Kitzman) Kreiger, living in a Prussian settlement twelve miles below the Upper Sioux Agency, testified that in the first two days of the war she saw her husband and one of her children killed. Another child died of starvation. She witnessed the mass killing and beating of other German settlers. In charge of eight children in all, her own and her husband's by a former marriage, she saw several of these taken from her. She herself was run over by a wagon and left for dead. She was later stripped of her clothing with a sharp knife and left naked and unconscious. She says she "took to eating grass, and drank water from the sloughs." She was eventually reunited with most of her remaining children.[84]

Ernestina Broburg, a sixteen-year-old girl from Norway, had been in Minnesota only one year when the outbreak occurred. She saw her mother shot to death and was separated from her father, whom she never saw again.[85]

Justina Cobitsche Boelter came to the United States from Posen, Prussia, in 1854. During the outbreak she discovered her mother-in-law dead on the floor of her house, beheaded. Boelter lived in hiding with her children for five weeks, eating raw potatoes. During that time one of the children died of starvation.[86]

Lavinia Eastlick and her family were among a party fleeing from the outbreak when her husband, eleven other men, and her six-year-old son were killed. She escaped with a fifteen-year-old son and her fifteen-month-old baby boy. Despite being "wounded in three places," Eastlick walked ninety miles in eleven days.[87]

MORAL VANTAGE POINTS The losses these women sustained were violent, intense, and personal. The moral sensibilities attributed to women while in safe havens often crumbled under the pressure of crisis. Whatever their character had been, it was now "vulnerable to erosion by uncontrolled events," what philosopher Martha Nussbaum calls "the fragility of goodness." Nussbaum finds the best of human lives vulnerable to the impact of "luck" or to what an historian might call the rush of events.[88] On the one hand, it is no wonder that these women could not see beyond these crisis points. They sustained great personal traumas. Still, if women have a sense of caring, why were they not able to see beyond their own crises and their own self-interest to see the world of other human beings also in crisis, especially *before* they themselves were at risk?

What is it about greed, war, and cross-racial and cross-cultural situations that blinds participants to any sense of another's justifiable grievances? What is it about the we-versus-they mentality in these situations that weakens moral judgment? If Minnesota's Christian women (and men) had true moral superiority, what happened to it?

White women out of their households on the frontier used the ethic of care in its narrowest sense. Their moral universe encompassed their immediate family, their property, and their racial stake in Minnesota. Few cared for Dakota women or men, their children, their prior claims to the land, or their neglect by the government. Perhaps few of the immigrant women understood the circumstances of their new-found relative wealth in what had been Indian land.[89] Of course, in the heat of warfare, when these white American and immigrant women were under fire, we would not expect clear moral vision. But we have little or no evidence of their sympathy for the Dakotas' situation *before* the siege began. Nor in their narratives and testimonies did they come to the defense of Dakotas *after* the U.S. military victory over the rebellious Dakotas. More typical were the following remarks.

Helen M. Tarble found herself unable to find any "noble traits" and refers to the Sioux as "red demons" who "bathed their cold hands in the blood" of those who had shown them kindness. She describes them before the outbreak as "cunning, deceitful, and treacherous." When she worte of them forty years later she called "the majority" of them "lazy and shiftless and very poor."[90]

Mary Schwandt wrote of her captivity as "my great bereavement." She said nothing about Dakota bereavement. Similarly, Jannette E. Sykes De Camp Sweet described the "web of fate" the Indians had "woven" about "their unconscious victims." She perceived herself and other whites as hapless victims, although she acknowledged that "those starving wretches" were "destitute" and "at Christmas time things looked very gloomy."[91]

And Urania S. Frazer White recalled with nostalgia the beauty of her first years along the Minnesota River before the land was, as she said, "overrun by savages." That this land was theirs did not occur to her. In a summer in which Sarah Wakefield noted Dakota children starving and eating unripe fruit, White described the Indians as plotting and "bloodthirsty," their "treachery" coming "to the surface." The day of the hanging she called the "day of retributive justice" for "some of the blood-thirsty savages." The moment of justice came for her when the trap "was sprung at the same instant, and thirty-eight bloody Indian villains were dangling at the ends of as many ropes."[92]

It appears in these examples that any sense of care is overwhelmed by a desire for retribution, by hatred, and by what appears to be a moral wall.

Sarah Wakefield and Moral Force

Sarah F. Wakefield was, among the captives, the only one of approximately one hundred women and men to come forward to testify for Dakota people.[93]

Why was Wakefield's moral vision different from those of others and what role did religion or gender play in it? Wakefield too went through crisis points. She sat behind George Gleason, a man her husband had charged with driving her and her two small children to safety. She watched as he was shot and killed. Hapa, who had killed Gleason, threatened to kill her and her children. She was held captive for six weeks. She was tormented by being told that her husband was dead. She and her children were almost killed any number of times. True, she was given special treatment by some Dakotas who recognized her as the wife of the doctor who had helped them in their battle with the Ojibwas in the summer of 1858.[94]

Even so, Wakefield saw, first, the importance of reciprocity as a Christian concept. Chaska, a Dakota man, helped her, as did his mother, as did any number of other Dakota women. She felt she must simply "do unto others." Second, she saw beyond her national and ethnic group and criticized the government for the causes of the war. She also blamed white traders who cheated Dakotas and mistreated Dakota women. She pointed out how the government contributed to Indian starvation before and after the war. She believed that Christian morality involved a serious religious and moral commitment. She believed further that it involved action. She held Christians, both men and women, to the standards they professed. She held ministers and Indians, men of both cultures, to a single Christian moral standard. She held her government, an avowedly Christian government, to this same Christian path.[95]

At the close of her narrative Wakefield says of the Dakota people: "Their reservation in this State was a portion of the most beautiful country that was ever known, and they had everything they wished to make them comfortable if they could have only stayed there; but a few evil men commenced their murderous work, and all has gone to ruin. I feel very sorry for many of my neighbors who for years have lived like the white man; now they are wanderers, without home, or even a resting place." She then tells of an Indian family that had recently passed through Shakopee. Recognizing them, she ran down to talk and bring them food. "For this," she laments, "I have been blamed; but I could not help it. They were kind to me, and I will try and repay them, trusting that in God's own time I will be righted and my conduct understood, for with Him all things are plain."[96]

Wakefield was not perfect. But she took risks for which she and her family paid the price, not the ultimate price the Dakota people paid—death on the high plains—but a heavy price nonetheless. Why? Because she believed in the most basic message of Christianity, that Indians as human beings should be treated as God's creatures.

It appears then that in the Dakota War, the moral standards of white women were neither necessarily "superior" nor "inferior." As a group, no maternal halo hovers above their heads. The traumatic effect of losses sustained by them and violence done to them apparently blinded many Christian women to their moral duty to defend the innocent and to look to the ultimate causes of Minnesota's predicament. The violence some of these women experienced was intense and horrifying. But for some, their economic stake in the homesteads their families had carved out of what were Dakota lands, and the lust of many Minnesota whites for the land along the Minnesota River, caused them and others caught in the war to say nothing in defense of the Dakotas, nor look to the real reasons for revolt.

In the ideology of True Womanhood that emerged in the period from 1820 to the Civil War, women were presumed to have a superior moral sensibility and a stronger religious sense than men. Perhaps these attributes pertained only if women remained cloistered in the home. But in claiming farms on a new frontier and in the midst of a war against their own people, perhaps understandably, rather than exhibiting care, some women became vindictive, while others limited their concern to their own families, having little interest in caring for those beyond their family circle.

In terms of a Christian moral conscience Sarah Wakefield was the exception, not the rule.[97] Why was she an exception? Was her New England heritage a factor here?[98] In the Dakota case, "doing unto others" was not the moral path taken by most white Minnesota mothers, nor even by some mixed-blood converts, whether captives or residents. Gestures of help more commonly came from Dakota mothers. Sad to say, it appears that for most women on both sides in Minnesota's racial and ethnic war xenophobia, economic self-interest, and national, racial, and ethnic identification all overrode both justice and care for others. The presumption of a special maternal moral sense then does not hold widely in the Minnesota case across American white, immigrant, and Native cultural lines.[99]

The issues of war, justice, and empathy across ethnic, racial, and cultural lines are among the most basic and significant ones of our time. Arguments for the special biological or even socialized sensibilities of women do not fully explain women's actions in the Dakota War. The Victorian presumption of white women's innocence and moral superiority did not hold. We might demand of them a moral vision for building a broader community, first by acknowledging their own pain and suffering and then by acknowledging the equally horrific and often more devastating pain and suffering of others. What is needed is not some special ethic of caring for women, but rather an ethic of care and justice among both sexes, all cultures.

Sarah Wakefield's narrative and its implications for both Native people and for our world of fragmenting national and ethnic allegiances make one wonder about human responsibility in a world of different and often antagonistic cultures. Centuries ago the prophet Micah asked,

> [A]nd what does the Lord require of you
> but to do justice, to love kindness,
> and to walk humbly with your God. [100]

In the Dakota case, as in other American frontier wars, white and Indian men died in huge numbers; women and children lived with enduring trauma. Native cultures came again and again to the brink of destruction. War is some basic kind of hell. *Nothing* is fair in war. In Sarah Wakefield's world, women and men across the cultures needed to do justice, love kindness. This before war—in her world and in our own.

CHRONOLOGY

1823

May 25:   John Luman Wakefield born, Winsted, Connecticut.

1829

September 29:   Sarah Brown born, Kingston, Rhode Island.*

1847

John Luman Wakefield, graduates from Yale Medical School, New Haven, Connecticut.

1849

Minnesota becomes a territory.

1851

July and August: Treaties of Traverse des Sioux and Mendota reduce Dakota lands in Minnesota by 24 million acres, ceding rich farmlands and traditional hunting grounds in the southern part of Minnesota to the U.S. government, leaving a ten-mile swath of reservation land for the Dakotas on either side of the Minnesota River.

---

*Sarah Wakefield's grandson, James Orin Wakefield, says a family Bible lists her birth as June 2, 1830. The Bible is not in his possession, and I have not seen it. I find the birth of a Sarah Brown in Rhode Island who corresponds in age to the one found in the Minnesota records as September 29, 1829. Why the name Butts appears on marriage records is unclear.

1852

Harriet Beecher Stowe publishes *Uncle Tom's Cabin.*

1856

September 27:	John Wakefield and Sarah Brown F. Butts marry in Jordan, Scott County, Minnesota.

1858

First child, James Orin, born to John and Sarah Wakefield.

Minnesota becomes a state.

John Wakefield treats Dakota wounded in the battle between the Sioux and Ojibwa at Shakopee.

Washington, D.C., treaty limits Dakotas to the southern side of the Minnesota River.

1859

John Brown's Raid on Harpers Ferry, Virginia.

1860

Second child, Lucy Elizabeth, sometimes called "Nellie," born to John and Sarah Wakefield.

Abraham Lincoln elected President of the United States.

1861

February:	Confederated States of America founded.

April 12:	The Civil War begins.

1862

June:	Dakotas come to the Upper Agency to ask for food and money due them from the federal government.

July 14:	About 5,000 Dakotas return to the Upper Agency to demand food and annuity payments.

August 16:	$71,000 in gold for the annuity payments arrives in St. Paul.

August 17:	Incident at Acton results in the death of five white settlers.

August 18:	Meeting of soldiers' lodge in Little Crow's village; members of Little Crow's Mdewakanton band attack the Lower Agency; attacks follow on the Upper Agency and on other white settlements along the Minnesota River; Sarah Wakefield and her two children, James and Lucy, captured en route to Fort Ridgely.

August 19: John Otherday moves Dr. Wakefield and sixty-one others from the Upper Agency to safety in Hutchinson, Minnesota; Col. Henry H. Sibley appointed to lead a volunteer force.

August 20: Attacks begin on Fort Ridgely.

August 23: Second attack on German colony of New Ulm.

September 2: War spreads north and west on the Minnesota River—battle of Birch Coulee.

September 23: Dakotas prepare to ambush Sibley's forces; approximately thirty Dakotas killed at the battle of Wood Lake.

September 26: Surrender of about 2,000 Dakotas to Sibley's forces; surrender of approximately 260 white and mixed-descent captives, mostly women and children, including Sarah Wakefield and her two children, at Camp Release; the rest of Little Crow's forces begin to move west into Dakota Territory.

September 28: Military commission trials of the 392 Dakotas begin at Camp Release.

November 5: End of the trials; 303 Dakotas sentenced to hang.

November 7: Uncondemned Dakota men, along with women and children, given military escort to Fort Snelling.

November 15: Dakota prisoners march with Sibley to camp west of Mankato.

December 5: Lincoln issues executive order for the execution.

December 11: Presidential message to Congress on Minnesota prisoners.

December 26: Thirty-eight Dakotas hanged at Mankato.

1863

January 1: Lincoln issues the Emancipation Proclamation.

General John Pope dispatches now General Sibley and Gen. Alfred Sully to Dakota Territory to search out escaped Dakotas.

May: Dakotas imprisoned at Fort Snelling become the first to be shipped out of Minnesota; several hundred men are sent to prison in Davenport, Iowa; other men, women, and children are sent to a reservation near Crow Creek on the Missouri River, Dakota Territory, where many die; most eventually are moved to the Santee Reservation in Nebraska.

November 25: Sarah Wakefield writes and publishes first edition of *Six Weeks in the Sioux Tepees.*

1864

Sarah Wakefield publishes the second edition of *Six Weeks in the Sioux Tepees* (date unknown).

April 9: Lee surrenders at Appomattox.

1865

President Lincoln is assassinated.

1865–67

Sioux War on the Great Plains.

1866

Third child, Julia E., born to John and Sarah Wakefield.

1868

Fourth child, John R., born to John and Sarah Wakefield.

1874

February: Dr. John Wakefield dies at his home in Shakopee.

1876

Sarah Wakefield moves with children to St. Paul. Custer's defeat at Little Big Horn.

1888–89

Sarah Wakefield moves to St. Anthony Street in St. Paul.

1897

James Orin Wakefield dies.

1899

May 27:   Sarah Wakefield dies in St. Paul.

A NOTE ON THE TEXT
AND ANNOTATIONS

THE text that follows is the second edition of *Six Weeks in the Sioux Tepees* (1864). As mentioned earlier, this is the longer version of Sarah Wakefield's narrative, corrected by herself and expanded within one year of the appearance of the first edition.

Wakefield herself complains here of the errors in the first edition as it was rushed into print. In this present edition I have further standardized the text, correcting inconsistencies of spelling and capitalization and adding letters that were erased or left out in the 1864 edition. Although Wakefield was given to a prolific use of commas and occasionally employed unusual syntax, I have generally left both punctuation and syntax intact, choosing to assert an editor's prerogative only when the prose reached a stage of annoying obfuscation. Although Dakota names may be spelled differently today, I have kept her spellings.

Annotations—by way of end notes—have been added to identify people, events, and archaic words and to provide the reader with more detail. In some cases they also identify historical and ethnographic references.

SIX WEEKS IN THE SIOUX TEPEES

A Narrative of Indian Captivity

SIX WEEKS IN THE

SIOUX TEPEES:

A NARRATIVE OF

INDIAN CAPTIVITY

BY

Mrs. SARAH F. WAKEFIELD.

Second Edition.

SHAKOPEE:
ARGUS BOOK AND JOB PRINTING OFFICE
1864.

Title page, Sarah F. Wakefield's *Six Weeks in the Sioux Tepees: A Narrative of Indian Captivity* (1864). Photo courtesy of the Newberry Library.

PREFACE

I wish to say a few words in preface to my Narrative; First, that when I wrote it, it was not intended for perusal by the public eye. I wrote it for the especial benefit of my children as they were so young at the time they were in captivity, that, in case of any death, they would, by recourse to this, be enabled to recall to memory the particulars; and I trust all who may read it will bear in mind that I do not pretend to be a book-writer, and hence they will not expect to find much to please the mind's fancy. Secondly I have written a *true* statement of my captivity: what I suffered, and what I was spared from suffering, by a Friendly or Christian Indian, (whether such from policy or other motives, time will determine.) Thirdly, I do not publish a little work like this in the expectation of making money by it, but to vindicate myself, as I have been grievously abused by many, who are ignorant of the particulars of my captivity and release by the Indians.

I trust all errors will be overlooked, and that the world will not censure me for speaking kindly of those who saved me from death and dishonor, while my own people were so long—Oh, so long—in coming to my rescue.

SARAH F. WAKEFIELD.

Shakopee, Minn., November 25, 1863

53

SIX WEEKS IN
THE SIOUX TEPEES

IN June, 1861, my husband was appointed physician for the Upper Sioux Indians, at Pajutazee, or Yellow Medicine.

The first day I arrived in the Indian country, I well remember. It was on Sunday, and as I landed from the steamboat, I could not help exclaiming, "Is it here where I am to live?" for all I saw was one log hut and about six hundred filthy, nasty, greasy Indians, and I wondered if I was really at what was called Redwood. But I soon heard that the buildings were upon the hill, some 500 or 700 feet above the river. When I arrived at the Agency I was disheartened, low-spirited and frightened, for the buildings were situated on a high prairie, and as far the eye could reach, was a vacant space.[1] I then felt as if I had really got out of civilization: but when on the following morning, I learned that we were going 30 miles further west, I was alarmed. We at last got ready, and a train of seven wagons, with many women and children started. We had in our wagons $160,000 all in gold, and we rode in great fear, for the Indians were grumbling all along the road because of the change in the administration.[2]

Although I was nervous, I enjoyed that ride, for a more beautiful sight than that prairie, I never have seen. It was literally covered with flowers of all descriptions; the tall grass was waving in the breeze, and it reminded me of a beautiful panorama. It seemed really too beautiful for Nature's picture. After riding a few miles we began to meet with annoyances, in the way of sloughs. After leaving the Lower Agency, we traveled ten miles, passing through Little Crow's village, and I little thought then what I should have to suffer in that vicinity. When we arrived at the Redwood River, we all exclaimed, "What a romantic spot!" Very high hills enclose the stream, while huge rocks are thrown around in the valley, giving grandeur to the scene. After crossing the river, we came in sight of a house, used by Government as a school-house for the Indian children. The house consisted of two rooms below and one above. In this Mr. Reynolds and family were already established as teachers, and here also was kept the only hotel, after passing Fort Ridgely, going west.[3] We only rested long enough to give our horses breath after ascending the high hills, and we were objects of much curiosity to the Indians while we remained, for they all gathered around to catch a glimpse of their new "Father" that had just been sent them.[4]

Our ride over the remaining twenty miles was very unpleasant, for the sun was very powerful, beating down upon us in our open wagons. We got along very well until we would come to a slough and stick fast in the mud, when all would have to get out, and then putting two or three extra horses to the wagon, we would be able to extricate it. It was all novelty to us and we enjoyed it, however the poor beasts suffered. After riding a few miles we could not see anything but the road that looked like civilization. It seemed like a vast lake—not a tree or a shrub to be seen. Soon, however, we came to what the driver said was an Indian mound.[5] I do not know whether it was such or not, but it was a very high elevation of land; and there, in the distance we could see our future home, which much resembled a fort, as flags were flying from many of the buildings in honor of our arrival.

We arrived at the termination of the road about three o'clock in the afternoon, and found we must go down and around very steep hills in order to get across the Yellow Medicine River. What a splendid sight was that, as we, after winding and turning in and round great bluffs, came out into the valley of the river. Here we found quite a large Indian village. The houses were all made of bark, and the squaws were cooking outside. It was really a pretty and a novel sight. The waters were rushing and tumbling over the many rocks, and the Indians, playing their flutes, made music quite pleasant to our ears. We found that we were to cross this river, and to ascend a hill 600 feet high, made it seem as if we were going up to some great castle, for we could see the tops of the buildings in the distance, and we all remarked that we enjoyed this as much as pleasure-seekers did their visits to the old castles and scenery on the Rhine. We reached the top of the hill without further inconvenience than having to walk nearly all the way. Very glad was I when we got to our home, for I was exhausted. I found that there were only five buildings there—four large brick, and one frame—and a small brick jail, in which to confine unruly Indians. The situation of the Upper Agency was beautiful, being at the junction of the Minnesota and Yellow Medicine Rivers. On the North side of our house was the Minnesota, and on the north side the Yellow Medicine River, being not more than eighty feet apart.

The first night passed there was one of horror to all, as we were ignorant of Indian customs any further than what we had learned from those who were camped around our town, and this night they were having councils and were talking, shouting and screaming all night, and we, poor, ignorant mortals, thought they were singing our death-song, preparatory to destroying us. Towards morning the noise lulled away, and we dropped to sleep, but not to sleep long, for soon came the tramp and noise of a hundred horsemen close to the house. The men all arose, prepared their arms, waited and watched, but no attack was made. What could be the trouble? [W]hy did they not make some manifestation? [W]hy were they silent—only that terrible tramping? At last one man, braver than the rest, went down, and, behold, —————it was our own horses, which had been turned out. They had come up on the platform to get away from the mosquitoes. This gives, in the beginning, an idea of many Indian scares. Many times we were needlessly frightened, but at last came one that was real, as our friends and our country know to their sorrow.

We found that there were employed at the Agency, for the benefit of the Indians, a blacksmith, farmer, and doctor; also, that there was a school taught by a half-breed named Renville, who had been educated in Wisconsin, and had returned to his home, his teacher following him back and marrying him.[6] They had many pupils, all Indian children. They professed to teach them all kinds of manual labor. The scholars were fed and clothed by [the] Government, the teachers feeding their own pockets more than they did the children's mouths. The hotel was kept by the farmer, and during our stay was a good house. We soon knew we could be very happy, although so far away from civilization. After being there a few days, we learned that three miles above us there was a missionary station, conducted by Dr. Williamson, a good Christian and an excellent man.[7] How I learned to love his family; while there they were so very kind to us all. The old man had been among these Indians 27 years, and had educated and converted many of them. Girls and boys brought up by them were equal in learning to white children of the same age. I have employed women educated by the missionaries who could sew or cook much better than girls of the present generation can do. Many persons say the Indian cannot be civilized. I think they can, but did not know it until I lived among them. I usually, on the Sabbath, attended the Dakota Church, and was much interested in their

Dakota women winnowing wheat at the Upper Sioux Agency, August 1862. Photo, Adrian J. Ebell, Minnesota Historical Society [E91.32/r8].

services.[8] Sometimes I would go to Mr. Riggs' Mission, which was situated about two miles beyond Dr. Williamson's, at a place called Hazelwood.[9] It was a delightful spot, and the rides to the place I enjoyed exceedingly. The scenery around Rush Brook was grand. Enormous hills—almost mountains—were on every side of this stream, and when a person was at the top and commenced descending, they would tremble with fear for awhile, but at last they would entirely forget all danger, while looking at the beauties of the scene. Away down between the hills, among the brush, could be seen these wild men roaming in pursuit of game, while their wives and children bathed in the stream, and from the top of the bluff they looked like babes, the distance was so great. I often wondered what an Eastern person would think, to ride through those woods, as we did, unprotected. I usually, after the first few weeks, went with my little boy, alone, to Hazelwood, often returning long after the sun was down, and very often passing through the Indian camp, which about the time of payment consisted of about five thousand Indians. I never knew one to be cross, but on the contrary were very kind and pleasant. I often was stopped and asked to take a puff from their pipes, or canduhupe, as Indian women smoke all the time, only when they are at rest.[10] When they cook they smoke. They

Thomas S. Williamson (center left with hat) and Dakotas in front of
Williamson's home at the Pajutazee mission, August 17, 1862. Photo, Joel E.
Whitney, Minnesota Historical Society [E91.7u.3].

have a long stem to their pipes, about two feet in length, and they will
sit on the ground, mix their bread, and bake it, the pipe resting on the
ground, the end in their mouths.

The first Independence Day I passed in the Indian country I
passed in great fear. A messenger came from the Indian camp in the
morning, saying that the Indians were coming down to make mischief;
they were angry because some of their old employees remained whom
they thought had defrauded them. We did not know what to do. There
were only 15 men there at that time, and it would be useless to try to
defend ourselves against thousands. Major Galbraith was absent, and
Major Brown (the former agent) was very much alarmed.[11] He proposed that we all should go to the jail and try to keep them off. In the
mean time he sent his son on horseback to Fort Ridgely, a distance of
45 miles, for troops. I think all stayed in the jail for many hours, except
Mrs. G——h.[12] She said her cooking must be done, as we had invited
all the mission people down for a Fourth of July party in the evening,
and if she was to die it might as well be at home as any place else; and
if we did escape we would all be rushing back for food. During the af-

ternoon a friendly Indian arrived and said they had postponed their attack until Major G—— arrived, as they wished to ask some questions before doing anything; so we were contented and had our dance. The Indians, however, sent down quite a number to guard our buildings, and would not allow any person to go out or in without questioning them. We danced that night, every moment expecting a shot from some of our Indian guards; but when we had eaten our supper, and we had invited some of the Chiefs in, and they [ate] for the first time, ice cream, it seemed to calm them down, and they came in and witnessed our dance with great pleasure. I think the Indians all took a fancy to me at that time, for I gave them something of all we had, took them around, showed them our rooms all ornamented for the occasion. They all said that the "Tonka-Winohiuca waste," meaning the large woman, was very good. [13] The next day Major G. came home, and they all came down, dressed up finely, for a council. They surrounded the Warehouse, which was a large, fortified building, on the West end of the Agent's house. [14] The Agent took his interpreter, and went up to one of the upper windows and talked with them. They wished for food immediately, and wanted to come in and help themselves. He told them they could not come in. They then began to complain of the Farmer, or Christian Indians. Said they were allowed in, and they every week got food, when they only got it once a year, and if the Farmers would be fed by the white men, and try to be like the whites, they should not have any money at time of payment, for it all belonged to them. They got very saucy, kept firing their guns up in the air, and beating against the doors. At last the Agent told them how much flour he would give them. They refused the quantity, saying it would not make a taste for each. He did not tell them that was all, but such was the case. The provisions had not arrived. Just as they were threatening him, some teams came up the hill, loaded with flour, and he told them they might have all they had; this was accepted, but they soon demanded what was first promised them; then they were satisfied, and after dividing it they went away, contented. That is the only way the wild Indian can be kept quiet, by just filling them with food; for if before eating they feel like fighting, they eat so ravenously that they have to sleep, and then forget all during their slumbers.

This was all of any consequence that transpired during the first year of our stay. The payment went off quietly, with the exception of a drunken Indian occasionally.

There were at Yellow Medicine, I believe, four trading houses, where were kept groceries and dry goods for the Indians, cheating the creatures very much. Indians would buy on credit, promising to pay at the time of payment. [15] They have no way of keeping accounts, so the traders have their own way at the time of payment. All the Indians are counted, every person giving his name, each Band by themselves. [16] At the time of payment they are called by name from the window to receive their money (which at the Upper Agency was only nine dollars to each person.) [17] As soon as they receive it the Traders surround them, saying, you owe me so much for flour. Another says you owe so much for sugar, &c., and the Indian gives it all up, never knowing whether it is right or not. Many Indians pay before the payment with furs, still they are caught up by these Traders, and very seldom a man passes away with his money. I saw a poor fellow one day swallow his money. I wondered he did not choke to death, but he said "They will not have mine, for I do not owe them." I was surprised that they would allow such cheating without retaliation; but it came all in God's own time, for at the Trader's was the first death-blow given in the awful massacres of August, 1862. All the evil habits that the Indian has acquired may be laid to the traders. They first carried the minne-wakan among them. [18] The Traders took their squaws for wives, and would raise several children by them, and then after living with them a number of years would turn them off. [19] It was the Traders who first taught them to swear, for in the Indian language there are no oaths against our God or theirs.

The first year of our stay was comparatively quiet, the Indians, after they were paid leaving us for their homes far away, with the exception of those who were farmers, and were living near us as neighbors. And I will state in the beginning that I found them very kind, good people. The women have sewed for me, and I have employed them in various ways around my house, and began to love and respect them as well as if they were whites. I became so much accustomed to them and their ways, that when I was thrown into their hands as a prisoner, I felt more easy and contented than any other white person among them, for I knew that not one of the Yellow Medicine Indians would see me and my children suffer as long as they could protect us.

In the spring of 1862, the Agent, accompanied by my husband and others, visited the Indians living near Big Stone Lake, "Lac Traverse" and that vicinity. They found the Indians quiet and well contented with what was being done for them, and they seemed much pleased with their visitors.

Before leaving, Maj. Galbraith told them not to come down until he sent for them, as he had doubts respecting the time of payment. He had not been home many weeks when they began coming in, a few at first frightened by some murders committed among them by Chippe-was.[20] Not long was it before the whole tribe arrived and camped about a mile from the Agency buildings.

Here they remained many weeks, suffering from hunger—every-day expecting their pay so as to return to their homes.

After repeatedly asking for food, and receiving none of conse-quence, they were told by the interpreter, who belonged at Fort Ridgely, and who accompanied the soldiers to Yellow Medicine a few weeks be-fore the arrival of the Indians, to break into the warehouse and help themselves, promising them that he would prevent the soldiers from firing upon them.

I think it was the fourth day of August, that the Indians com-menced hostilities at Yellow Medicine. We were much surprised early Monday morning, to hear them singing and shouting so early in the day. Soon they came driving down the hill toward the Agency, dressed out very finely, and as we thought, for a dance; but we were soon convinced they meant mischief, as they surrounded the soldiers, while part of them rushed up to the warehouse and began cutting and beating the doors in pieces, all the while shouting, singing, and throwing their blan-kets around them like wild men as they were—driven more wild by hunger.

I was with my children up stairs in my own house, my husband's office being in the building connected with the warehouse. I was very much frightened, and called to my girl to fasten the gate and come in and secure the lower part of the house. Soon the Indians commenced filling our garden and all adjoining. In a short time they surrounded our house and some came to the door, and rapped violently. I caught up a pistol and went down stairs, opened the door, and inquired as calmly as I could what they wanted. They wished axes, and filled the room and followed me around until I gave them all we had. I expected they would kill me, but I knew I could raise an alarm with my pistol before they could get my children. But they offered no violence, and departed qui-etly; all they cared for was food—it was not our lives; and if all these Indians had been properly fed and otherwise treated like human be-ings, how many very many innocent lives might have been spared.

In ten minutes time, after surrounding the warehouse, the door was opened and they were carrying out flour. Soon, however, the sol-diers came to the building, and the Indians were obliged to evacuate the premises, but not without many ugly threats and savage looks. The Agent went out and counciled with them, and asked them to give up their flour; but they refused and he was compelled to give them all they had taken and much more before they would leave. That night there was little sleep at the Agency; all were expecting an attack before morning.

Just at sunrise the next morning, a friendly or Christian Indian came and told us that the Indians were preparing to make an attack; as they had succeeded so well the day before they would try again. We all knew that matters would be different a second time, as the soldiers intended firing upon them if they came again.

Several families concluded to go down to the Lower Agency, which was thirty miles below us—myself and children being among the number. We remained a week and while I was there I attended Mr. Hindman's church, and was much pleased with the behavior of the Indians during service.[21] Little did I think while I sat there that my life and my children's would so soon be in danger, and that our deliverer would be one of those wild men that were listening with eager attention to God's word. Surely the missionaries have done good; for where would the white captives now be if the Christian Indians had not taken an interest in their welfare? Monday, August 11th, I returned to my home, my husband coming for me, and saying that the upper Indians had left very quietly, Major Galbraith giving them goods and provisions, and promising to send for them as soon as their money came. I went home with the determination of preparing my clothing for a journey East in a few days, as we were fearful some of the Indians might return and would be troublesome, stealing and begging all summer.

Many who read these pages may not understand about the Indian payment. I will say a few words respecting it: In June these people usually come in off the lands which they have sold to the United States, some coming many hundreds of miles; and if the money is not ready, they expect to find food for themselves, procured at the expense of the Government, as that is part of their treaty. As soon as they are paid they leave, and very few are ever seen until another year has passed away. Last year they came in at the usual time, although many knew they should not come until they were sent for, as before mentioned. But they were all in, and it was no use trying to send them back again, and of course they must live; and the prairie is a very poor place to find any kind of game, and five thousand persons could not long stay where they were without something to support nature. What dried meat they brought was soon eaten, and in a few weeks they were actually starving; the children gathering and eating all kinds of green fruit, until the bushes were left bare. They had several councils, asking for food which they did not get. Many days these poor creatures subsisted on a tall grass which they find in the marshes, chewing the roots, and eating the wild turnip. They would occasionally shoot a muskrat, and with what begging they would do, contrive to steal enough so they could live; but I know that many died from starvation or disease caused by eating improper food. It made my heart ache to see these creatures, and many times gave them food when I knew I was injuring ourselves pecuniarily; but I always felt as if they were God's creatures, and knew it was duty to do all I could for them. I remember distinctly of the agent giving them dry corn, and these poor creatures were so near starvation that they ate it raw like cattle. They could not wait to cook it, and it affected them in such a manner that they were obliged to remove their camp to a clean spot of earth. This I witnessed. It is no idle story, and it is one of many I witnessed during my short stay among them. I often wonder how these poor deceived creatures bore so much and so long without retaliation. People blame me for having sympathy for these creatures, but I take this view of the case: Suppose the same number of whites were living in sight of food, purchased with their own money, and their children dying of starvation, how long think you would they remain quiet? I know, of course, they would have done differently, but we must remember that the Indian is a wild man and has not the discrimination of a civilized person. When the Indian *wars,* it is blood for blood. They felt as if all whites were equally to blame. I do not wish any one to think I uphold the Indians in their murderous work. I should think I was insane, as many persons have said I was. I wish every murderer hanged, but those poor men who were dragged into this through fear I pity, and think ought to be spared.

When on my way home from the Lower Agency the soldiers passed us on their return to Fort Ridgely. I was much surprised, and expressed my regret that they should leave so soon, and felt that was a very unwise proceeding; but the Captain assured us there was no longer any need of them, as the Indians had all departed.

That night the Agent had a war meeting, and a company of volunteers were raised taking about forty men away, the Agent putting his name down first. They left in a few days, passed through the Lower Agency, causing the Indians assembled at that place to think their "Great Father" had not many men left or he would not have taken them away from the Agency. They were very angry because the Agent did not stop and have a council with them, and give them goods and provisions, like the upper Indians. There has always been a jealousy among them, as they thought the upper Indians were better treated than they, and this feeling, with what the traders told them, exasperated these men, for they were suffering nearly as much as the upper Indians. The traders said to them they would get no more money; that the Agent was going away to fight, and they would have to eat grass like cattle, etc.

The Indians always blamed the agent for not giving them their goods, and repeatedly said if he had done so they would have scattered back to their homes satisfied, and this awful massacre would not have occurred; but he was deceived respecting these men. He thought they were just like white men, and would not dare to rise, living as near as they did to the Fort; but he must now see his mistake in not explaining matters to these Indians; for only two or three days passed before they commenced their murderous work. I don't think he did this willfully; it was through ignorance. He did not understand the nature of the people he had in his charge.

Sunday, the 17th of August, the Indians killed some people in Acton, and on returning to Little Crow's village, said to him, what shall we do?[22] He said they should go to the traders, kill them and all other whites; that they must clear the country of all the whites so they might live. Monday, the 18th, they began their work of destruction at an early hour, killing the traders in their stores; when this was done they began their work of destruction in general. The wine and spirits found in the stores added drunken madness to the madness of despairing vengeance, and soon the Indians were dancing wildly about the dying embers of what had lately been the stores and homes of the traders; then they passed on, killing everything they met. Their savage natures were aroused, and blood-thirsty as wild beasts they raced and tore around, beating, crushing, and burning everything they had no use for.

Soon the news came that the soldiers were approaching, when they started for the ferry; but that bloody battle has been many times described, where so many of our kindred were murdered by these savage fiends, made so by liquor and revenge. This affair at the ferry seemed to cheer these people on, and they soon spread over the country, murdering all that were within their reach. How these savage creatures abused the traders after death is not generally known. They broke open the safe at one store, and commenced pelting the dead bodies with gold, filling their mouths and ears, saying to them, you have stolen our money, now take all you will. Some of the Indians acted quite decently, and buried many things belonging to the missionaries, to save them from destruction. Monday, soon after dinner, my husband came in and said I had better get ready and go down to Fort Ridgely that afternoon, instead of waiting for the stage. Mr. Gleason had come up on Saturday and wished to return and had no conveyance, and had offered to drive me and the children to the Fort if my husband would let him take our horses and wagon.[23] (Mr. Gleason was clerk in the warehouse at the Lower Agency.) At two o'clock we started. I felt unusually sad, I remember going from room to room, taking a final look. My husband grew impatient and asked me what I was doing, and I made some excuse. I knew he would ridicule me if I told him how I felt. As we were starting he said, "Gleason, drive fast, so as to get to the Fort early." I asked what was the hurry, but he made me some answer that satisfied me then, but many times while I was in captivity I thought of our conversation. I inquired of Mr. Gleason if he had a pistol; he said he had, but it was not so; for after his death no weapons of any kind were found upon him. We drove to the traders, and Mr. Garvie came to the wagon and said he had heard bad news; that the Indians had been killing some persons over in the "Big Woods," and that the Indians were all getting ugly, and at the Lower Agency they were having councils to determine whether they should kill the whites, or if they should give up this country and leave for Red River.[24] He also said that our Indians were only five miles away and were having councils to decide upon the same subject.

I was anxious to go back, as we were only under the hill from the Agency, but Mr. Gleason made great sport of me. He said he had doubt that the upper Indians would make trouble, and he was in a hurry to get home, for he would send four or five hundred lower Indians up to fight for the whites. He then told me that my husband had heard these reports and that this was his object in sending me away in such a hurry; that as soon as we got away from Yellow Medicine all would be right. Poor misguided man! All this day these lower Indians had been committing these awful murders, and, we, not knowing it, were going down into their country for safety. I rode in great fear that afternoon. I was very sad and sorrowful. Death seemed hovering near me. Not a person or a living object did we meet as we rode, and I remarked to Mr. Gleason many times that there was something wrong below, as usually we were constantly meeting teams on that road.

Mr. Gleason was very lively, more so than I ever knew him. He would laugh, sing, shout, and when I would chide him and tell him how I felt, he would say I was nervous, and told me he would never take me anywhere again. I endeavored to have him return with me but he said I would live to see the time I would thank him for taking me away. He tried every possible way to make me feel contented: but it was of no use. I had strong feelings of evil, and it was a presentiment of what was to happen. As we got to the mound which is half way between the two Agencies, we could distinctly see the smoke of the burning buildings. I said to him that the Indians were destroying the Agency. "O, no;" he said, "it is the saw mill or the prairie on fire." I became frightened, and tried again to persuade him to return. I was so excited I could not sit still, and endeavored to jump out of the wagon. Then he really scolded me, saying it was very unpleasant for him to have me act in that way. Very well, said I, go on; they will not kill me; they will shoot you, and take me prisoner, "Why," said he, "who are you talking about? The lower Indians are just like white men; you must not act so hysterical;" for I was now crying. Very soon we came in sight of Mr. Reynold's house, which was near the Red Wood river, twenty-two miles from Yellow Medicine. He said to me, "You now see you have been acting very foolishly, for 'Old Joe's' house is standing." But for all, I could not look around [for there was] only that great body of smoke. As we drove toward the house he looked at his watch, and said: "It is now a quarter past six; we will eat supper here at 'Old Joe's,' and at eight o'clock we will be at Fort Ridgely." The words had barely passed his lips, when, as we were descending a little hill, I saw two Indians coming toward us. I said, "Mr. Gleason, take out your pistol;" but he said "be quiet! they are only boys going hunting." I then said, "hurry up your horses." Instead of doing so he drew in the lines, and spoke to them, asking them where they were going.

I will here [describe] the wagon we were in and the way we were sitting: It was an open wagon, with two seats. Mr. Gleason was sitting on the front seat, directly before me, my boy sitting at my right hand, and my baby on my lap. As the Indians passed the wagon, I turned my head, being suspicious, and just then one of them fired, the charge striking Mr. Gleason in his right shoulder, whereupon he fell backwards into my lap, crushing my baby against me. He did not speak, and immediately the savage fired again, striking him in the bowels as he laid across my lap. He now fell backwards out of the wagon as he turned at the fire, bringing his back toward the side of the wagon. O, what a sight was that for a mother! and what were my thoughts, for I suppose I should be shot very soon. As he fell, the horses ran furiously and the Indian who did not fire ran and caught the horses. As he came up, he asked me if I was the Doctor's Wife. I said I was. He then said, "Don't talk much; that man, (pointing to the one that shot Mr. Gleason,) is a bad man. He has too much whiskey." As soon as he had quieted the horses, he came to the wagon and shook hands with us, and one ray of hope entered my heart; but it was soon dispelled, for when we turned around where poor Gleason lay groaning and writhing in his death agonies, I saw the other Indian loading his gun, and I expected every instant to be launched into eternity. When we rode up near I begged him to spare me for my children's sake, and promised to sew, wash, cook, cut wood, or anything rather than die and leave my children. But he would not speak, only scowl hideously—Chaska, the good man, urging me by his looks to be quiet.[25] Just then, Mr. Gleason spoke for the first time, saying, "O, my God, Mrs. Wakefield!" when Hapa, the savage one, fired again, killing him instantly.[26] He stretched out and became calm without a groan. Now, as I write it, all appears plain before me, and I can scarcely hold my pen. I never can feel worse than I did that night. I passed through death many times in imagination during my stay on that prairie. It now seems so plain before me I cannot keep from trembling; but it must be told. In a moment after poor Gleason breathed his last, Hapa stepped up to the wagon and taking aim at my head, would have killed me but for Chaska, who leaped toward him and struck the gun out of his hands. I begged Hapa to spare me, put out my hands towards him, but he struck them down. I thought then my doom was sealed, and if it had not been for Chaska, my bones would now be bleaching on that prairie, and my children with Little Crow. Three or four times did this demon try to destroy me, when Chaska would draw him away by his arm, and I could hear him tell him of some little act of kindness my husband or myself had shown them in years gone by. But all Hapa would say was, "She must die; all whites are bad, better be dead." Who can imagine my feelings, exposed as I was to the danger of being shot every moment, and not knowing what might be my fate if I was spared.

I think those men disputed about me nearly an hour, Chaska trying every inducement to influence him in my favor. How many and varied were my thoughts! I felt as if death was nothing if my children were dead; but to die and leave my petted ones to the fate that might be in store for them was agony. I could see them left to starve to death, or partly murdered, lying in agony, calling for their dead mother. Father in heaven, I pray thee impress this upon the minds of an ungenerous world, who blame me for trying to save the man who rescued me from death when it was very near! After a long time, Hapa consented that I should live, after inquiring very particularly if I was the agent's wife. He thought I was; but Chaska knew to the contrary for he had been at my house in Shakopee many times. He often said that if Hapa could have got the Agent's wife, he would have cut her in pieces on her husband's account.

Chaska and Hapa got into the wagon, leaving poor Gleason on that prairie alone with his God. Unfortunate man! If he only had listened to my entreaties, his life might have been saved, and I been spared six weeks of painful captivity. I rode in much agony; I knew not where I was to be taken, or what might eventually be my fate. I turned and took a last look at Mr. Gleason's remains; his hat was slouched over his face, his dog looking pitifully at him, and just as the sun went down, I bid farewell to him forever, Chaska telling me not to look any more, for Hapa was very cross, and said if I turned around he would kill me now.

Hapa sat facing me all the way, pointing his gun at my breast; and he kept saying, "Those children I will kill: they will be a trouble when we go to Red River." But Chaska said, "No! I am going to take care of them; you must kill me before you can any of them." Chaska was a farmer Indian, had worn a white man's dress for several years: had been to school and could speak some English, and read and spell very little.

Hapa was a wild "Rice Creek Indian," a horrid, blood-thirsty wretch; and here can be seen the good work of the Missionaries.[27] The two men were vastly different, although they both belonged to one band and one family; but the difference was this: the teaching that Chaska had received; although he was not a Christian, he knew there was a God, and he had learned right from wrong.

After riding a few miles, we reached the Indian encampment, consisting of about two hundred persons. As they perceived who I was, their laments were really touching to my feelings. They proved to be old friends of mine. Six years previous to my living at the Agency, I had lived in the town of Shakopee.[28] In the winter there were camped around the town this same band that I was now among. Not a day passed but some of the Indians were at my house, and I had always pitied them, and given them food. But at the time of the battle between the Chippewas and Sioux, near Shakopee, many Sioux were wounded and my husband attended them, extracting bullets, etc., and they often said he saved many of their lives; and now I was with them they said they would protect me and mine.[29] When they assisted me in alighting, many of the old squaws cried like children. They spread down carpets for me to sit on, gave me a pillow and wished me to lie down and rest. They prepared my supper, and tried every way possible to make me comfortable; but that was an impossibility. They promised me life, but I dared not hope, and felt as if death was staring me in the face.

I had not been there long, when a half-breed approached, saying he felt very sorry to see me, that I would probably be spared a few days, but would at last be killed, as they had sworn to kill everyone that had white blood in their veins. He did very wrong, for he knew better than to try to increase my fears. He was a great rogue.

After the old squaws had given the children supper, Chaska said I had better go with him to a house where there was another white woman, for my children would take cold sleeping on the prairie, as they would not put up their tepees that night.[30] I was afraid to go, and asked the half-breed what I had better do. He advised me to go; he said; "Chaska is a good man, and you must trust him, and you will be better treated." He then gave me some very good advice; he said as long as I was with them I must try to be pleased, and not mistrust them; make them think I had confidence in them, and they would soon learn to love and respect me, and that would be my only way of prolonging my life, which advice I followed, for I never gave them a cross look. If they were telling any of their plans or of their exploits, I would laugh, and say, "That is good; I wish I was a man, I would help you." When they were making preparation for a march or for going to battle, I was as busy as any. I prepared the meat for the warriors, pounding it in leather, and then putting it into skins I would press it, and make it ready to be carried around their waists.[31] I helped paint blankets, braided ribbons to ornament the horses, and in short tried by every way to make myself useful, hoping by such conduct to gain their friendship. I knew I could in that way conciliate them, and a different course would have caused different treatment.

I started with Chaska, leaving my trunk of clothing in the wagon, carrying my baby and leading my boy, Chaska carrying my satchel. We walked about a mile, part of the way through the woods. I was suspicious, but I kept up with him, and tried to talk of the heavy dew which was falling, not letting him know I was frightened. He stopped at a tepee, I suppose to show his prisoner. While I was there the Indians brought in Mr. Gleason's clothes, and his watch, which was still running. I looked at it and saw it was just eight o'clock, the very hour he said he would be at Fort Ridgely. The crystal was broken in the center, with a bullet, I suppose. The Indians were having great sport over his empty pockets. He had no pistol: he had deceived me. It was not safe at any time to go without firearms, and I many times wonder why he did such an unwise thing. There was a white woman at this tepee but I did not learn her name. She was a German, and her greatest trouble seemed to be the loss of her feather beds. She had seen her husband killed, but that was very little compared with her other losses. This woman, through the night, would moan and sob, and at last she would break forth into a wail saying, "All my five feather beds gone I picked

the feathers myself in Old Germany, and now they will not give me one
to sleep on." She said that after the Indians killed her husband, father,
sister and brother, they were about to kill her, when she said, "Don't! I
will give you my house, everything I have, and I have much money." So
they spared her. She also said, that, in their hurry to get away with her
and her goods, they forgot the money, and after crossing the river, she
was compelled to return alone and get the money, which was secreted.
I think it very strange they did not murder her, for they had all she possessed, any way. She was a sickly woman, having a babe only two weeks
old. She declared she had not been abused by the Indians. She said they
were very kind. She only mourned the loss of her feather beds.[32]

They asked me to take off my hoops which I did.[33] I think I should
have cut off my right hand if I could have saved my life by so doing.

We only stayed here a short time, and then went to a barkhouse
where I found another woman. They had a good fire, plenty of candles,
and made me as good a bed as could be expected. I was told to lie down
and go to sleep, as we would start for Red River in the morning; but
sleep was far away from our eyelids that night and many others. After
Chaska had made us comfortable, he left us in charge of some old
squaws and boys, telling me to go to his mother's tepee in the morning,
and tell her to give me a squaw dress, saying I would be more safe in
such an attire. The German woman and I managed to get through the
night, but she spoke very poor English; still she was white.

No one can imagine the confusion of an Indian camp when the
braves come home victorious; it is like Bedlam broken loose. Hour after
hour we sat listening to every footstep, expecting death every minute.
Guns were firing in every direction; women were mourning over their
dead, and the conjurers were at work over the sick or wounded, all
tending to increase the confusion.

Morning came at last, and as the sun arose, the Indians began to
leave us. They were going to attack Fort Ridgely. Now as it was quiet, I
went to Chaska's mother, and soon I was changed from a white woman
to a squaw. How humiliating it was to adopt such a dress, even forced
by such circumstances! This day, Tuesday the 19th, was an extremely
hot day, and I began to suffer. My bonnet was gone, as well as everything I possessed. I thought I would be sun-struck, for we were kept on
a constant move. The squaws would get frightened, pack up, and off we
would go; when soon they would hear different stories and we would
rest awhile. Many, many times that day, was that repeated. Once they
heard that the Sissetons, or Upper Indians were coming, when the old
women rubbed dirt into my skin to make me look more like a squaw.[34]

Surely I did not look like a white woman. I had the pleasure of viewing myself, for they had a large glass belonging to Mrs. Reynolds resting against the fence, and the squaws were having a fine time admiring themselves.

I sat down by the roadside, and while we were waiting for news from the Fort, I tried to disguise my children. I rubbed dirt all over my boy, but his white hair would betray him. I tore off the shirt of my baby's dress, took off her shoes and stockings, but did not rub dirt into her flesh, for she is naturally of a very dark skin, and the squaws said she looked like a papoose after I had her made rugged.

During the morning, an old squaw called Lightfoot came and sat down by me, and said they were going to kill me in a few days but were going to keep my children, and when they were large, their Great Father would give them much money for them.

I became nearly frantic. I had thought of this all night, and I determined I would kill them rather than leave them with those savages. I ran to a squaw, begged her knife, caught up my little girl, and in a moment would have cut her throat, when a squaw said it was false. What I suffered, let every mother imagine, when you think of my trying to cut my child's throat myself. But my thoughts were like this: if my children were only dead and out of trouble, I could die willingly; for I supposed my husband was dead, and I cared not to live only for my children.

About four o'clock in the afternoon, Chaska's mother came into her lodge, saying that a man was coming to kill me; and she caught up Nellie, my baby on her back and told me and my boy to hurry. She stopped at the bark house where I had stayed the night before. She told an old man her story, and he said "Flee to the woods." She gave me a bag of crackers and a cup, and we ran to a ravine. It was very steep, and the banks were like the roof of a house. When we got to the bottom she hid me in the tall grass and underbrush, and bidding me sit still, left me saying she would come in the morning.

I have passed through many trials and different scenes, but never suffered as I did then. God so willed it that a storm arose as the sun went down, and a furious storm it was. No one, unless a Minnesotan can judge of our thunder showers. But I did not fear the storm, for I felt that God had sent it for my benefit; still we suffered from the effects of it. The rain and mud washed down upon us from the side of the hill, wetting us completely through in a few minutes. I had one blanket and tried to keep my children warm with that. I had in my satchel a small bottle of brandy, and I put it into my bosom, and during that night, as my children would awaken, I would give them some in their drink; it kept them from taking cold. When I recall that night my heart beats with fear.

Surely God gave me strength, or I would have died through fear for I am by nature a very cowardly woman;—every leaf that fell during that night was a footstep, and every bough that cracked was the report of a gun. My nerves were so weakened that my heartbeats would sound like some one running, and I would frequently hold my breath to listen. Muskrats looked like wolves, and as they crawled around me in the darkness, I thought they were wolves, and they were going to devour me. I sat all night, my feet in a running brook and I dared not stir for fear I might make some noise that would lead to my discovery, for I could hear the Indians racing around, firing guns, singing, hooting and screaming.

Many persons who may read this may think I was foolish in giving away to my fears, but you cannot tell what you would do or how you would feel; for I many times now, when I think of it, think I was foolish; still I have no doubt I should feel the same under like circumstances. My children would awaken often, and I would hush them, telling them the Indians were near, when the little darlings would lay close to me and tremble with fear. I cannot tell how I lived through that night, but I know God was with me. I passed the time in prayer. I thought of my husband lying murdered in his blood, and my friends in a like manner: then I would beg of God if they were alive to spare them. I know He heard me, for we all know how narrowly they escaped.[35] Can anyone imagine how I suffered? No! they can not. I now do not realize my agony. Just for a moment, my readers, think of a woman at any time lying in the woods alone all night. We would all pity a person who was so exposed. Then again think of me, being down in those deep, dark woods, I knew not where I was, or how long I might stay. I felt that my bones might at some future day be found; but O, what thoughts were mine that awful night—when the elements of Heaven were all at work and devils incarnate were rushing around, seeking whom they might devour! My little boy would awaken at times and say, "Mamma, take me home; put me into my own little bed: What do you sit here for? O, mamma, do go home; my father will not like his boy to stay out of doors all night." I would then in whispers tell him what the trouble was, and he would say, "I forgot about the Indians; I will be still; I have been asleep and dreaming."

After a flash of lightening I would pray for the next to strike me or else save me to meet my husband. I never knew how to pray before; but I had no one to call upon but God, and I knew He could save me, and I begged and plead with Him all that night, as a child would with a father. Never can I forget His goodness; never can I cease praying to One who brought me out of such dangers.

Morning came at last. Sorry was I to see the light. I felt sure we would now be discovered and our fate sealed. Hour after hour passed, still the old woman came not, and it was all quiet where noise had prevailed during the night; nothing could be heard but the singing of the birds and the running of the brook.

I now began to think she had forgotten me and removed, and that my children and myself would be left to perish in the ravine. I knew I could not climb those banks alone, and our bag of crackers would not last long. I now saw starvation, as well as other evils, staring us in the face. Our situation was truly horrible. We were completely covered with mud, and now the sun was shining, the mosquitoes were very numerous. My children's faces were running with blood from their bites, but the darlings were as quiet as if they had been at ease, for their fears were so great they did not notice their stings.

After waiting several hours I saw the old woman coming, and I was overjoyed to see her. We laughed, cried, and I really think I kissed her, for I felt as if our deliverer had now come. She took Nellie on her back and I tried to get up, but found I could not stand, from the effects of sitting so long in one position, and my limbs in the water had chilled my blood and stopped circulation. But the old woman rubbed me and while doing so said the men had gone who were going to kill me, and I must try to walk to her tepee, and she would give me some dry clothes and some coffee. She said they had removed across the Redwood River, and this accounted for the stillness in the morning.

When I was able to walk we started, she carrying both children up the bank, and then helped me up, for I had not strength to get up alone. I was completely prostrated. I had not eaten a morsel since I left home on Monday; now it was Wednesday. The exposure and fright, combined with nursing a child twenty months old, had reduced my strength exceedingly. When we got up to the bark house, the old woman got me a cup of coffee and some painkiller, which revived me greatly. We walked about three miles, stopping at every tepee for some coffee or tea, and she would make me sit down and warm myself, for I was shivering with fear and disease.

At last we came to the Redwood river, and we commenced fording it, the water in some places being up to my shoulders—the old woman still carrying my baby, and I my boy where he could not walk. But the child was as brave as a man, and ran along through the woods that morning with scarce a murmur, the bushes tearing his little bare feet until the blood ran. Occasionally he would exclaim "Oh! Oh!" I would shake my head and speak in Dakota, that the Indians would hear him, when he would remain quiet, when I knew the little fellow was suffering extremely, for I could not bear my own sufferings without a groan occasionally.

We did not go in paths or roads, but through the tallest and thickest brush, and among all kinds of berry bushes entwined together, with grape vines and ivy. We did not stop to part them, but tore through like wild beasts when driven by fear, and of course we tore our flesh badly. I am completely covered with scars which I will carry to my grave.

Those persons who think I prefer Indian to civilized life, ought to travel as I did last summer. It was because I was carried through so much by that family to save me from death; and what is more, that I was anxious to do all I possibly could for them when they needed assistance.

After crossing the river we arrived safely at their encampment. They had no tepees up, but were getting dinner, each family by their wagon.

When I came to where my home was to be, I felt comparatively happy. I had endured so much the past night, that even squaws seemed like friends, and they proved to be good, true friends. Poor women! how I pity many of them! driven from their good homes, their families broken up and divided. Many of them are as much to be pitied as the whites, and many of them no more to blame.

When I had rested awhile, they gave me my dinner, dry clothes, water to wash my children, and prepared me a bed to lie down.

I learned that Chaska [was] still absent; that he and his mother were living with Hapa and his wife, she being a half-sister of Chaska. Her name was Winona, and I feared her, for she was like her husband, the murderer of poor Gleason.[36] She tried every way to make me unhappy when Chaska was absent, but was very good in his presence. I will here say that my trunk of clothing, which was very valuable, she appropriated to her own use, and would not give us anything to wear, and the old woman would go around and beg when my children needed a change of clothing. She would not give me a pin to fasten my sacque, and I was compelled to sew it together.[37] She took my embroidered under-garments, dressed herself in them, and then laughed at me because I was so dirty and filthy. One day her boy had a collar (which I prized very highly,) in the dirt, playing with it. I asked him to give it to me. He did so, but she took it from me and tore it in pieces, and then threw it into my face. One day I told Chaska I must have a sacque, for mine was so dirty, when she gave me some cloth to make one. A shower coming up soon it got wet, the colors all faded out, and he saw it was not good, and he was angry. He caught her by the hair, slapped her in the face, and abused her shamefully. At last I coaxed him to desist, but he said she was a "Sica-Winohinca," meaning a bad woman. She took my ear-rings from my ears and put tin ones in their place, and dressed herself in mine; cut up my silk dresses and made her boys coats to tumble around in the dirt with. All little articles, such as miniatures, etc., she would destroy before me and would laugh when she saw I felt sad. I would like to be her judge, if she is ever brought within my reach. She and her husband are now with Little Crow.

After lying quiet about an hour, I was surrounded by squaws, who commenced talking about some evil that threatened me. The old woman said there was a bad man who would kill me, and I had better go to the woods again. I told her I could not, and I must die, for I was completely exhausted. I arose and looked north where the excitement was, and saw a hut made of green boughs, and women led into it by an Indian wearing a white band on his head; presently I would hear a shriek and see female clothing spread out, and what we all thought were bodies put into an ox wagon, and then driven off. A German (the only man who was spared, except George Spencer,) came where I was hidden under the wagon, and said we were all to be killed in a short time.[38] He said the squaws were much excited, and wished him to hide in the woods, but he thought it useless. The old woman soon came back, and said: "You must not talk, and I will cover you and your boy up with buffalo robes and the tepee cloth," and then taking my baby again on her back, kept marching backwards and forwards, as if she was guarding me.

I made up my mind to die. I knew if Chaska was only near he would save me. I conversed with my boy in a whisper, charging him to try and remember his name and his sister's, and tried to impress upon him the necessity of always staying with her and taking care of her, so that if his father or uncle should be alive, he might some day be able to find them.

Several times I raised the tent cloth and inquired what the news was, but the woman was crying and would only say, "Chaska dead, and you will die soon; that man is a very bad man." I cannot describe my feelings. I know I prayed; that I begged God to save me from the savages; sometimes I cried, then I would be calm, and once I began to sing. I thought I would not die despairingly; I would try and go to my death cheerfully. At last I felt perfectly happy, and I believe if I had died then, I would have died a Christian. I had bidden the world farewell. My husband I thought dead, and all I had to live for was my children, and I was in hopes they might go with me. I said to my little boy, who was not quite five years of age, "James, you will soon die and go to Heaven." "O, Mamma! I am glad, ain't you? for my father is there, and I will take him this piece of bread," (which he was eating.) Poor child! he was not old enough to know how he was to reach that happy land.

I asked Winona how we were to be killed, and she said "Stabbed," pointing near the heart. I dreaded death in that way, for I was fearful we might suffer some time. While I sat there thinking of my sad fate and of my friends in the East, and how they would feel when they heard of my death, I thought I heard a neigh from our mare that Chaska had gone away on. Soon I heard her mate, who was tied near, respond, and I felt a sudden thrill, as if my preserver had come. In a moment the tepee cloth was raised, and Winona said, "Come out! Chaska has come; it is all right now." I did not need a second invitation. I went out and surely there he stood. He shook hands, and said: "Don't be afraid; he will not dare to hurt you while I am near; if he comes near I will shoot him." O, how happy was I! My life was again saved, and by him. Had not God raised me up a protector among the heathen? Have I not reason to bless His name, and thank the man and his family for all their goodness towards me and mine? for my little children would now be motherless if he had not taken care of me.

The remainder of this day I passed quietly. That night a violent hurricane arose, upsetting our tepee, which had been put up soon after Chaska had arrived, and we were compelled to go under the wagon and lie down on the wet grass the remainder of the night, while the rain poured down upon us. What a scene was that, as we arose from the wet ground. In every direction could be seen the fires, as the hurricane had upset nearly all the tepees, and it looked like some picture I had seen where witches were holding their revels; for, crooning over the fires, were the old women of the families, who seldom ever sleep in the night, but sit smoking their Kinnikinnick until day begins to dawn; then, with a prayer to the sun, they retire.[39] I have often in the night sat and watched these old creatures, as they smoked, talked and cooked, until I really thought their magic spells were really at work upon me; for they would take the form of very devils, in the midnight hour, over their fires, singing and moaning in their half-stupid state. I don't know as this is always so. It might be they were fearful of losing their prisoners. Such nights as these I have described helped my already diseased imagination, until at times I was nearly frantic, for with all this was the continual firing of guns, and I really thought every one sent some poor creature into eternity, and expected every minute my turn would come.

Thursday, the 21st of August, the Indians were up very early, getting ready for an attack upon the Fort. Chaska was going, and he said he was afraid to leave us where we were, for fear Hapa might return and kill us. He told me I had better go with him to his grandfather's, who lived in a brick house about a mile from where we were. Soon the wagon was ready, and myself and children and the old woman were riding away. Before leaving, Winona painted my cheeks and a part of my hair. She tied my hair (which was braided like a squaw's down my back) with several colored ribbons and ornamented me with fancy colored leggins, moccasins, etc. My children were painted in a like manner; then she gave me my blanket, and told me to start. Who would have known me to be a white woman? I sometimes forgot I was, when I would look around me and see how I was living. If I had been without children I should not have stayed there and submitted to being painted and dressed out in such a manner. I should have tried to escape, and if I had died in the attempt, well and good: I should have had no children to leave. As it was I dared not try, for I knew I would be discovered and then death would have been certain. I know that after the first few days a person might have escaped, and I often tried to urge young girls to do so. I know I could have got away if my children had been large enough to walk; but as it was I could not, for mine were too large to carry, and not able to walk but a very little ways. We were at liberty to go where we pleased, could go to the river, go after plums, or from tepee to tepee, if we wished, and often as I went down to the Minnesota River for water, I would stand and form plans respecting my escape. The water was so low that we could ford the river, and once across I know a person alone could have secreted themselves, and got back to the settlements without detection.

The prairie that morning was alive with Indians, all in high spirits, and confident of taking Fort Ridgely. They were either over dressed *or else not dressed at all;* their horses were covered with ribbons, bells, or feathers, all jingling, tinkling, as we rode along, the Indians singing their war songs. It was a grand but savage sight to see so many great powerful men mounted on their bedecked animals, going to war. Many of the men were entirely naked with the exception of their breech cloth, their bodies painted and ridiculously ornamented. I little thought one week before when passing over that road, that I should be in such a train, and the train on its way to kill my kindred. We arrived at the house of his grandfather just at sunrise. It was a very cool morning, and a fire which they had in the stove cooking breakfast, was really comfortable. There were several tepees around his house. I found, after alighting from the wagon, that I was with some of my best friends in the Shakopee Band. An old squaw called by the whites "Mother Friend," was there, and glad was I to see her. Chaska went soon after I got my breakfast, saying he would stop for us at night. I passed this day in great anxiety. We could hear the cannon at the Fort, and see the smoke from the burning buildings. We were camped just at the head of a small ravine opposite the Fort, only a few miles above, and we could see the Indians as they fired, run down into the woods and reload, then rush backwards and forward. I expected every minute some one would return and in their rage destroy us, for they were nearly all drunk at this time, and nearly every day some one would look at us saying they are going to "Pa Baksa," meaning you will have your head cut off. We heard many different stories relative to the fight; sometimes we would hear that the Indians were all killed and that the whites were coming; then the confusion that would ensue was such, that many times we fled to the ravines and hid ourselves in the bushes.[40] The squaws were very cowardly, and I was needlessly frightened many times by them. My children feasted this day, one family having enough nuts, candy, maple sugar, &c., to open a confectionery store.

I never shall forget the kindness of old Mother Friend that day; she would not let me stay in the old man's house, but must pass the day with her. She made my boy new moccasins, brought water and washed my sacque, carried my baby around on her back, and did all in her power to lighten my sufferings. She said when the old grandmother called me to dinner, "No, she is my child, she has given me cooked food in her tepee in Shakopee; now she must stay and eat bread with me." Her daughters tried every way to amuse me, and would tell me that when their father came home he should take me down the river in a boat, but although the father was kind, he never offered to take me down as they promised.

Just at sunset a messenger arrived, saying the Indians were going to stay all night, and that a chief was coming to kill us white women, there being two besides myself in that camp. I was told to flee to the woods again, and Eagle Head, Chaska's grandfather, said he would go with me.[41] He was an old man, nearly eighty years old. Mother Friend said I should leave James, as he was asleep, and she would take care of him. The old man took his gun and I my baby on my back; we started in great haste for the woods, which we roamed all night from dark until daylight, never stopping only long enough to nurse my baby; when we would hear them shouting, we would dive deeper into the gloom. The old man could not keep up with me, but I would wait for him, and he would say, "Stop, I am tired; I will die." As day began to dawn, it became quiet, and we came out of the woods on to the bottom lands of the Minnesota River. He said he would go back to camp, but he must hide me first, for he dared not take me back until he knew how matters were. He proposed hiding me in a hay stack, saying he could pull out the centre and put me into the middle and then cover me up. He did so and left me to sit, as I thought, for a short time; but hour after hour passed. It was noon, and I thought I should suffocate or die with thirst. My baby kept worrying for we started without supper, and the child was hungry; while she was nursing it would pacify her, but made me very weak, for, not having eaten anything, I had very little nurse for her. I sat hours that day nursing her, when I thought I should faint with the constant drain upon me. I could hear water running but dared not come out of my hiding place, for I had seen Indians very near me twice that day. I nearly choked my child when I heard Indians coming, and she was fretting; I clasped my hands around her throat until she was black in the face, for I knew her cries would lead to our discovery and death. Poor baby, she tho't her mamma very unkind, for she would look so pitifully when I would do so, but it saved our lives.

I sat that way all day until sunset. I thought night never would come. I was miserable on account of my boy. I knew he would cry himself sick, for he never was away from me a night in his life. How I blamed myself for leaving him, but I expected when I left to return in a few hours. Where; oh! where, was my child, I would ask myself. I was fearful he would scream and cry and some ugly Indian would kill him. Soon after sunset I heard a voice and a footstep near, but I dared not speak. Presently the old white head of Chaska's grandfather appeared, and he said, "Come out," at the same time throwing the hay off of me. I was rejoiced to see the old man. He said I must not talk loud for some of the Indians were ugly. I asked for drink or food—he said I must wait until I got to the tepee. It was some time before I was able to stand, as I had sat in one position eighteen hours with my feet drawn up under me. As soon as I could stand, we started and I found I had got to walk several miles. I did not think I could live to walk but strength was given me.

I inquired for my boy but he knew nothing about him. All the gloomy thoughts I had indulged in during the day again arose in my mind, and I was almost sure he must be dead, or he would know where he was; still I knew Mother Friend would save him if possible.

As we walked along we passed through a muddy piece of ground and I dipped up the filthy water in my hands and drank and gave my child. It was refreshing, but I think a dog would refuse to drink such water at ordinary times: but my mouth was parched with thirst. Many times during the day I reached my hand into the middle of the hay stack and would find some moist hay, and would draw it through my lips to try to moisten that awful dryness of my mouth and throat.

We walked I think four miles; every one I met I inquired about my child, but could hear nothing of him. I at last arrived at the tepee. He was not there, but Winona soon came in, saying that he was very near. Presently he came in; what a joyful moment for a mother's heart. He rushed into my arms and cried, as if his little heart would break, "O mamma, I thought you was dead, and I was left alone with the Indians. I have cried until I am sick. O, dear mamma, have you got back? Do kiss me, and keep your arms around me. I thought you and Nellie had gone to Heaven and left your boy all alone." He said he did not awake until morning, and Mother Friend told him I would be back soon. After he had his breakfast Winona came and carried him up to her tepee on her back. He said he had cried so much that Roy, a half-breed, had taken him to see an ox killed, "But, mamma, I thought you might be somewhere shot like the ox, and it made me cry more."

I could not get him out of my arms that night. He clung to me in his sleep, and trembled with fear if I made an attempt to lay him down. I sat all night and held him, and watched the stars through the opening in our tepee, and wondered if his father could see us in our captivity.

I learned after a while, that the Indian who threatened us came and as we were all secreted, they told him we were at the large encampment. They searched around and went to the woods, but it being dark, and they lazy and tired, concluded to wait till morning to put their threats into execution, which it appears was not death, but what would have been worse. [42] Now, my readers, what say you? Am I not indebted to those friendly Indians for my life and honor? What would have been my lot that night if they had not interested themselves to save me, you can imagine. I can never express my gratitude to those who befriended me when in such danger; let people blame me if they will, God, who knoweth all things, will judge me, and I will wait and bear all the reproaches the world may cast upon me, knowing that with Him all will be well.

The next day being Saturday, we arose early, as it was reported we would leave for Yellow Medicine in course of the day. The morning passed quietly, the Indians deciding to remain till Tuesday. Soon after dinner, an Indian called Chaska out. He returned very soon, saying, "I wish I could kill all the Indians." I inquired, what was the trouble. He said an Indian was drunk in the next tepee, and was going to shoot all the white women in our camp. He told his mother to close the teopa, or door, and watch. Just then I heard the report of a gun, and a woman shrieked, "I am shot! I am shot!" The old woman said he had shot her through the legs, as she sat outside the tepee.

Chaska appeared much alarmed. He sat down on the ground, told me to sit back of him, taking my children in my lap; and if the Indian came he must shoot through him before reaching me. We sat in this way a long time, until his mother said he had passed away from our tepee, when she tore up the back part of our tepee, and taking Nellie on her back we again fled to the woods. She found a good place, covered us up with boughs of trees, and left in a hurry, not saying when she would return. I sat awhile, and hearing running water I thought I would follow it, and perhaps I might reach the Minnesota River, I took Nellie on my back (as I had learned to carry her in that fashion) and we followed the brook some ways, until a large tree which had fallen across it completely impeded our progress. I was obliged to stop or retrace my steps, and I decided to remain, as it was a very good hiding place. We sat in the water until sunset, when I heard the old woman calling, "White woman! where are you?" She had been where she had left us and was much frightened when she found us gone. She followed our tracks along the stream, and appeared delighted to see us again. I am sure I was delighted to see her honest old face, and as she took my baby again on her back and arranged my blanket around my shoulders, and scattered my hair over my face to conceal my countenance, I could not refrain from giving her a good kiss. I learned to look upon that woman as I would upon a mother, and I hope some day to be able to do something for her. She said that a large number of Indians had just come in from the Fort, bringing many mules, and that now was a favorable opportunity for me to go back home, as they were so excited over their plunder. We were near our tepee, when she discovered the Indian we were in fear of, and she hurried me into a tepee and covered me up with robes, telling me to lie as quiet and as flat as I could; then the squaws threw their packages on to me, and I looked like a great bundle of goods. The old woman left, telling the squaws to give the children food. Soon some Indians came in and asked whose children they were. They said their father and mother were dead. I expected my little boy would speak and say who he was, for he could speak Dakota very well; but the child showed the good sense and reason of a man all the time we were in captivity. In a few minutes the very Indian who had threatened me, came and inquired if a white woman was there. They said no. I can assure all who read this that my heart beat with fear and trembling, for I did not know these squaws, and I did not know but they might betray me. While I lay there an Indian lad came and sat down on me, thinking I was a bundle of goods piled up against the tepee. Fortunately he sat there only a short time, or I should have been smothered. I could not take a long breath for fear he would notice the motion of my body. Soon Winona came in and told me to hurry back. We went home and had a good supper, and glad was I to lie down and rest, for my feet had become so sore that I could hardly walk, and they were very painful. My left foot was entirely covered with sores, poisoned by weeds, and constantly irritated by running through the prairie grass.

I always felt safe when I was in Chaska's tepee, for he always cautioned me when he went away not to go out unless I was obliged to, saying that no man dared enter the tepee of another person and commit any violence, unless it was a drunken person. There was no need of cautioning me, for I had no disposition to run around as I had traveling enough that was necessary. Many of the white prisoners were roving from morning until night, and would often wish me to accompany them, but I always refused. I could not be happy in any place, and if I could sit with the old woman and have her wash my feet and attend to the sores, [it] was all I cared for. I felt as if this was my home, and I stayed there all the time I was in captivity, and was much better treated than any other female on that account.

I thought I was better off staying there attending to my children than I was roving around gossiping, all the time in danger of being shot down by the Indian soldiers; for of all the places for gossip I ever was in, that Indian camp was the worst. There were several half-breeds that spoke good English, that reported every word spoken by us white women, to the Indians, and so things were exaggerated and misconstrued, going through so many lips and different languages. I always took particular pains to speak in favor of the Indians, many times upholding them in their undertakings, because I knew it would all be repeated again to the Indians; and my sole object was while there to gain their friendship so as to save my life, I hoping that God would pardon me for any deceit used in such a way. I little thought every word would be remembered and told to my injury. I trust God may forgive those that have done this grievous wrong, as fully as I do; for the worst is for themselves.

Saturday night I slept very well until near midnight, when Hapa came home, the first time since my captivity. He was drunk, as usual. He awakened all by his drunken actions, but I little thought of his daring to molest me in the tepee in the presence of all the family. I pretended to be asleep, but soon he asked where the white woman was. He said, "Come here! I wish to talk with you."[43] I dared not speak or move; I thought now he will kill me, as a drunken Indian knows not what he is doing. I asked the old woman in a whisper what I should do; she said, "Lie still! Chaska will not let him hurt you; he will go to sleep soon." But not he, for he soon arose, and, with knife drawn, came towards my place, saying, "You must be my wife or die!" I said, "Chaska, come here; he will kill me!" He said, "Be still! I will take care of you," whereupon he arose and came toward me, asking Hapa what he wanted. He said, "She must be my wife or die!" Chaska said, "You are a bad man; there is your wife, my sister. I have no wife, and I don't talk bad to the white women." I told Chaska to let him kill me, only kill my children first. He said, "Stop talking then." He turned to Hapa, who had his knife drawn and was still flourishing it, and said, "You go lie down; I will take her for my wife, for I have none." Hapa said, "That is right; you take her, and I will not kill her." Chaska said, "Yes, as soon as I know her husband is dead, I will marry her;" but Hapa said I must be his (Chaska's) wife immediately. I did not know what to do. I caught hold of the old woman's hand, but she said, "Don't be afraid; Chaska is a good man; he will not injure you." Then Chaska said, "You must let me lie down beside you or he will kill you, he is so drunk. I am a good man, and my wife is in the 'spirit world,' and can see me, and I will not harm you." He came and laid down between his mother and me, and Hapa went back contented, and was soon in a deep drunken slumber. When Chaska thought he was asleep he very quietly crawled back to his own place, and left me as he found me. My father could not have done differently, or acted more respectful or honorable; and if there was ever an honest, upright man, Chaska was one. He has suffered death, but God will reward him in Heaven for his acts of kindness towards me. This was not the only time he saved me in a like manner. Very few Indians, or *even white men*, would have treated me in the manner he did. I was in his power, and why did he not abuse me? Because he knew that it was a sin; he knew that I was a wife, and he always intended to restore me to my husband, and often said he would give me up as he took me.

It was constantly reported and many believed that I was his wife, and I dared not contradict it, but rather encouraged everyone to believe so, for I was in fear all the while that Hapa would find out we had deceived him. I did not consider the consequences outside of the Indian camp, for I had my doubts all the while of my getting away. I supposed if I was ever so fortunate as to get back I could explain all, never once thinking people would consider me a liar, as many call me. Mine is a sad case, after all I have passed through, to receive now so many reproaches from those that I thought would pity me.

Sunday morning our tepee blew down again, and we were obliged to sit under the wagon and wait for the old woman to go to the woods and cook our breakfast, for the wind was so high they could not cook on the prairie. I was visited this day by a number of white women. They said they had heard I was married, and asked me if that was my husband. I replied that I supposed my husband was dead, and turned the conversation; for there were many near who could understand all we were talking about. These women went away and said I acknowledged it. Now this is the truth, and I am very sorry that women would do such a thing towards one of their own sex.

Sunday afternoon, I think, they decided to kill the prisoners, for Chaska came home soon after the Indian soldiers came in from the war path, and said something in a whisper to his mother, when she turned to me, saying, "Sica! sica! bad! bad!" Presently she got me some stockings and new pair of moccasins, washed my feet, and put them on. Then she started for the woods, telling me to let James go with her. He started to go, when I caught a look from Chaska, that seemed as if he blamed me, whereupon I started after him, caught him in my arms, and carried him back to the tepee. The old woman was very angry. I don't know what was the matter, but I always thought she was going to take him away that he might not see me murdered. This was very near night! She talked with Chaska, and told me to go inside the tepee. He soon left on horseback. It was with strange and conflicting thoughts that I laid my children down to rest that night, for I was sure my end was near, for they always dress the feet clean when a person is about to die.[44]

I had been in bed, (or what was called my bed, consisting of two strips of carpeting, two blankets and two pillows,) when Chaska came in with two Indians I never saw before, and said I must take my children and go with him. I asked where, and what was the matter. He said he would sometime tell me. I got ready, awakened my children, and we started. I knew not what was in store for me, still I trusted him and went along. Chaska carried James and I Nellie, and the two strange Indians walked on each side as a guard. It was very dark; a drizzling rain was falling, and here was I, at the mercy of these men, going I knew not whither; but as I had always found Chaska truthful and honest, I could not feel as I might otherwise. We walked a long way; left our encampment far behind us, and still we went on, and not a ray of light was visible. I began now to be suspicious, but he would only say, "Keep still!" We at last came to a small encampment, and he took me to his aunt's tepee, and told her I should stay there. They whispered together some time, and she looked at me very sadly. He left, saying he would come again in the morning. I never learned why I was carried there, I presume some danger threatened. Surely I was well watched and cared for by these people. Could white people do more? About this time I heard that my husband was dead. The Indians returning from Yellow Medicine said he was shot; then his head was cut off; also that all the rest of them were massacred in some horrible manner. O, what thoughts were mine! I felt that all worth living for was gone. I had just as soon died as not then, for I had always had some hope that he was spared, and would eventually have me rescued. Now I had nothing but my children. Would they be long spared? I could not tell; but God saved us all. Great thanks I return to Him for His goodness.

The Indians were as respectful towards me as any white man would be towards a lady; and now, when I hear all the Indians abused, it aggravates me, for I know some are as manly, honest, and noble, as our own race. I remained at Chaska's aunt's, who was a widow, all the next day. Towards night he came, and soon after his mother, and she said I must go; that the Indians were coming, and the next morning we would certainly start for Yellow Medicine, on our way to Big Stone Lake.

When we were going home, I saw an Indian who exclaimed, "There is the Doctor's wife." I smiled, and the old woman said, "Hurry on; he is a Sisseton, and will kill you." I was not afraid, as I knew the Sissetons would take care of me, and longed to go to Yellow Medicine. I knew the Sisseton chiefs would never allow Little Crow to kill me.[45] He was constantly threatening us all, and myself in particular. He was determined at times to destroy me, I being the only one of the Yellow Medicine people that fell into his hands, and he very often said I should die because they escaped. This caused me more trouble than any other woman there.

I remember one day, while I was still at Redwood, that a half-breed said there had been a council, and that all the whites would be killed very soon. I sent for Shakopee, the chief of the Band I was with, and when he came, I asked him if I was to be killed.[46] I told him if he would only spare me that I would help kill the other prisoners. I also promised never to leave his Band, and that I would sew, chop wood, and be like a squaw. I was so frightened that I really did not know what I was saying, nor did I care; for all I thought of was, if I can only live a little while longer, and get away, my husband, if living, will not care what promises are made, if his wife and children were saved.

It was awful the promises I made to kill my own people, but I was nearly crazy, and was expecting the soldiers to come very soon, and wished to live to see them. Many unthinking captives, hearing me make such remarks, have since published it to the world, causing people to believe I really meant all I said. Being naturally timid, and afraid of death under any circumstances, I looked upon such a death with horror. One day the old woman seemed much worried about something, I could not understand what. Chaska was away. Soon I heard guns firing, and I imagined they were shooting the white women. Now this I am about to write, was all imagination, to show people how my mind was a great part of the time.

I sat under the wagon this day, and near us was an ox-wagon and I sat and watched that wagon all day, imagining that it was full of dead bodies, and there being buffalo robes over the bodies, I could not see them, but could see their long hair hanging from under the robes. In [the] course of the day Winona came in with a piece of skin, and I thought as she laid it up to dry, it was to put around my throat, after it was cut. Now this was a piece of the ox (the sinew) they were to sew with; and the hair that I thought was human, was from the buffalo robes. Such a day as I passed! I suffered as much as if it had been real. I often wonder that I was not entirely deranged.

The night before we started for Yellow Medicine there was but little rest. The women were packing and the men preparing for battle, as the report came that the soldiers were coming. Just as it got light they started. My boy was sick with bowel complaint. I was forced to take off his pants, and not having any others, he traveled without anything on except a shirt and a little waist that held his pants up.

I had no moccasins allowed me that day, for squaws go barefoot when traveling, and I had to do likewise. Although they were in a great hurry, they did not neglect to paint my cheeks and ornament my hair. They were anxious to look fine, as they were going up into the Sisseton country. When the train started, in every direction, as far as the eye could reach, were Indians, all hurrying for the Redwood crossing. The old woman became much excited, and said I must hurry, as the Sissetons were coming and would kill me. That day I had my baby to carry, as the old woman had about eighty pounds to carry on her back. Such noises and confusion I never heard. My boy was crying, "I cannot walk

Mission refugees from the Williamson and Riggs missions near the Upper Agency, August 21, 1862. Sixty-two refugees from the warehouse, including John Wakefield and Henrietta Galbraith, crossed the Minnesota River to St. Paul and went 120 miles in five days and four nights, escorted by John Otherday, a Christian Dakota. Photo, Adrian J. Ebell, Minnesota Historical Society [E9145 r19].

so fast." Nellie would slip down nearly to my feet, and she would cry, and the old woman would fret because I could not keep her on my back, squaw style. If I stopped she would scold, and say I must go on. When we got to the river we found it full of teams, some fast in the mud, here a horse floundering in the water, there a boy trying to regain his footing; then you might see a horse with poles attached and an old woman up to her knees striving to urge the beast through; but the noise and confusion excited beasts as well as men, and I was fearful we would be crushed to death, for the Indian soldiers were galloping in every direction, firing their guns, not minding and not caring on what or where they tramped. Fortunately the river is not deep in summer. If it had been many of us poor females would have drowned. We were all more or less wet. I had my baby on my back, my boy by my hand, and it was very difficult endeavoring to keep myself from being drawn down by the current, for the water in many places was up to my shoulders, when I would have to take my boy in my arms, making quite a burden for a person not accustomed to such labor. When I was striving to get through, an Indian rode up to me and asked, "Where are you going?" I replied, "To Yellow Medicine." He said, "You are the Doctor's wife?" I said, "No, I am an Indian woman," for the old woman just whispered, "He is a Sisseton." He laughed and said, "I know you! you must not tell lies! you are not an Indian woman, your eyes are too light." When we got up the bank after crossing the river, where Mr. Reynolds' house once stood, this Indian, with two others, stopped near the ruins and called me to him. He leaned forward and whispered, "I am Paul; don't you know me?[47] You must go with me to my tepee." This reminds me of how frightened the Indians were just before leaving this neighborhood. They said that an old woman every night came to that (Mr. Reynolds') house, made a bright light, and they dared not go near there. They thought it the spirit of some one they had murdered, for after a little some of them said they would burn the building, which they did; but they continued to see her every night, sitting on the walls of the cellar. At last they said it was Miss Jane Williamson, for they knew her by her singing, and they were going to catch her.[48] I afterwards learned they had her secreted, but it was false, for she escaped with her brother's family. The light they saw was the moon's rays on the glass; but the poor superstitious beings thought they had offended some of their Gods, and this was a mark of their anger.

I knew Paul very well at Yellow Medicine, as he was a farmer but he was disguised in his Indian costume, so I did not recognize him again. He was very anxious I should ride, but I dared not attempt to ride thirty miles on a mule barebacked, when I never rode a horse with a saddle. My little boy knew him very well and was anxious to go with him. I said to the child, "You will cry when night comes for me because I shall walk, and not get to Yellow Medicine in two days." "No, no, mamma, I will not cry. It will kill me to walk so far; do let me go with Paul."

I asked Chaska, who had just come up, if I had better try to go with Paul. He talked with Paul a few minutes, and then said I could go if I wished to, but that Paul wanted me as a wife, and had been for several days trying to get a white woman. He also said that Paul had told him that my husband was alive; they had all made their escape from the Agency the morning after I left. What glorious news was that for a wife who had mourned for her husband as dead. I laughed, cried, and acted like a wild person. I could have danced for joy; my body as well as mind felt lightened. I felt now as if I must live and try to save my children. A new impulse was given me from that hour.

I told James he might go with Paul, for Chaska had advised me to let him go, as our load was so large he could not ride. He said as he started, "I wish you would go too, mamma," and seemed a little sorry I had consented to let him go. I now can see his little bare legs hanging down against the black ones of the Indian, and his white face looking so pitiful as he rode away. How many times that day I regretted that I let him leave me; sometimes I would think it might not be Paul and that I had been deceived, and probably I would never see him again. I saw him in all kinds of danger. I thought he might be sun-struck, riding that extremely hot day without a shade for his little head.[49] I was looking in all directions for his body. I suffered so much in my mind that I did not realize my bodily sufferings. The more I thought, the less hope I had of ever seeing him again; but then I thought that God could shield him from danger as well away from me as with me, and uttering a prayer in his behalf, I felt more calm and quiet, knowing he was in God's care.

I wish it was within my power to describe that procession as it moved over that prairie. I think it was five miles in length and one mile wide; the teams were very close together, and of every kind of vehicle that was ever manufactured. Nice coaches filled with young Indians, dressed up in all kinds of finery, the more ridiculous the better they were pleased. White women's bonnets were considered great ornaments, but were worn by men altogether. White crepe shawls were wound around their black heads; gold watches tied around their ankles, the watches clattering as they rode. The squaws were dressed in silk short gowns, with earrings and breast-pins taken from the whites.

It made my heart ache to see all this; still I could not keep from smiling at times to see how ridiculously they were used by these poor savage creatures; they looked indeed more like a troop of monkeys than anything human. Ox carts, chaises, baker's carts, peddler's wagons, all well filled with these creatures. Occasionally you would see the faces of the white children intermixed with the Indian children. Sometimes you would see a cow with poles tied to her back Indian style, and such a rearing, tearing and plunging was never seen before.[50] It was ludicrous in the extreme, and many times I laughed until I could scarcely stand; for very often in their plunging they would upset some squaw who had all her possessions on her back, and out would roll a baby, a dog, bread, sugar, and sometimes flour, all mixed together, with a great part of her wardrobe. I saw a very nice buggy, with an Indian pony attached, that never felt a harness before, and such antics never were witnessed. Everything was ornamented with green boughs: horses, men, women, and children. United States' flags were numerous, and many times it looked like "Uncle Sam's" camp. The noise of that train was deafening; mules braying, cows (poor animals) lowing, horses neighing, dogs barking and yelping as they were run over or trodden upon, children crying, kittens mewing, for a squaw always takes her pets with her; and then to increase the confusion, were musical instruments played by not very scientific performers, accompanied with the Indians singing the everlasting "HI! HI!" All these noises, together with the racket made by Little Crow's soldiers, who tried, but in vain, to keep things in order, was like the confusion of Babel.

I traveled in great distress barefoot, trotting along in the tall, dry prairie grass. In some places it was five feet high. My feet and legs were cut by the grass switching and twirling around them as we drove through, regardless of the many prairie snakes we tread upon. I was obliged to keep up with the other *squaws*, and they will trot as fast as a horse.

At noon, we stopped for dinner, which consisted of crackers, maple sugar, and good cool water. Chaska, when seeing my feet, said I must ride, for the skin was all off from one foot, and both were running with blood. His mother washed them and cleaned roots and wrapped them up: and when we started I was provided with a seat on the load and drove the horses the rest of the day. With what feelings I passed poor Gleason's body no one knows.[51] He was stripped of his clothing, except his shirt and drawers; his head had been crushed in by a stone. Now I was on this road going toward my once happy home, now desolate and destroyed; and he whom I was last with on that road was lying there dead, to be gazed at and stoned by these savages. I could not help rejoicing that my bones were not there also. How I wished for power to punish Hapa on that spot, although I must say he never looked towards the remains of his victim; perhaps his conscience smote him for what he had done.

We did not travel many miles after dinner, as the report reached us that we were pursued by white soldiers. What a scattering there was! All order was gone. All made for a little thicket, for nearly every one knows that this is the Indian's battle ground. Here were made preparations for a fight. Guns were discharged and re-loaded, bullets were run, powder flasks filled, and every man that night was ready for action. We camped two miles away from water, and I thought I would perish with thirst, but soon Chaska came in bringing a large bag of plums which refreshed me. What thoughts passed through my mind as I sat there under the trees with these people. My husband I knew not where he was. My boy gone I knew not whither, as I still had doubts of Paul. I felt sometimes as if I would be carried to Yellow Medicine and be murdered in sight of my home. I felt sure Chaska's family would protect me as long as they could, but every day we heard reports further respecting the disposal of us prisoners.

They had during my stay among the Indians a Soldiers' Lodge, where all business was transacted.[52] The Indian soldiers always go there on returning from battle and report. As soon as they can they send out a man who cries the news, whatever it may be. Every few days, as the Indians would come in, we would hear the cry, "White women to be killed now very soon; they eat too much; we are going away and they cannot travel; they had better die at once." This, of course, kept our minds in a perfect state of frenzy. I do not know how I lived with my nervous, excitable disposition; but there was One above who was strengthening me, or I should have fallen by the wayside.

The Indians did not put up many tepees the night we camped here; nearly all slept in or under their wagons, to guard their horses or goods, for they were in constant fear of some evil—sometimes Chippewas, Sissetons, or white men. They did not enjoy their plunder very much nor very long. We started very early for Yellow Medicine. Soon we came in sight of Major Brown's house. Where now was all this family with their elegance and comforts? in an Indian's tepee, their home destroyed, and their goods scattered! As we went further, I could see our houses at the Agency. They looked just as they did when we left, as the buildings were not burned until Little Crow's soldiers came up; they were in fear the soldiers would come up and occupy them as forts—

they being all of brick. What a loss there was to the country by Sibley not hurrying on his forces, for all our furniture remained good for three weeks after the people fled. When the people fled they left every thing; the Indians soon burst open the houses, robbed them of all kinds of food and such things as they could use in a tepee, leaving all large furniture as they found it. Major Brown's family, who were taken near Redwood by Little Crow's soldiers, were taken back by their relative Akepa, and when I got up to Yellow Medicine were occupying my house.[53] His son's wife was confined in my bed-chamber, and was quite comfortable there. The next day, however, she had to travel, for as soon as the lower bands went up they drove everything before them. When we got to the top of the hill I had to get out and walk, as the hill was very steep. We crossed the Yellow Medicine River. How different everything looked from what it did only one week before. All the wooden buildings belonging to the traders, which were in the valley of the Yellow Medicine.

Soon we were obliged to rise the hill on the opposite side, as the Agency is situated on a hill six hundred feet above the river; it was just at noon, the sun pouring down on my head until I was nearly mad with headache and excitement, for I lost the old woman, and Winona would not wait for me, and I had to run to keep up with her, as she would say, "If you stop the Indian soldiers will kill you." After rising the hill we waited two miles before we stopped. We then camped for the day. We stopped very near Other Day's house about two o'clock; not a shade of any kind for my head; I thought I must die before I got rest or water.[54] While sitting on the grass with my sick child, I heard Good Thunder, or Horton Waste's wife say she had water.[55] I went to her and begged for a drop for my child, who was endeavoring to obtain nurse from me; "No," said she, "white woman, get it yourself." She had some little boughs put up to screen herself. I sat down in the shade, but she soon drove me away. I was surprised, for they were *Christian Indians*. But I afterwards learned that Hapa and Good Thunder were great friends, and were, of course, cross to me because he was. They eventually occupied our tepee, and divided my clothing between them, Mrs. Good Thunder cutting up seven of my dresses in one day, all the while laughing because they were so large. My sufferings on that prairie, without shade or drink, cannot be described. I had not yet seen or heard anything from my boy; if I could have had him with me I could have born all other trouble patiently.

About this time the old woman came, and some trouble arose between her and Winona about some shot that was lost, Winona accusing the old woman of stealing them; they were very abusive and at last

Winona threw a tin kettle at the old woman, and she left, saying she would not stay any longer with her. When Chaska came I told him, and he said he would leave; that Hapa was all the time threatening me and my children because they ate so much. He said, "You go to my grandfather's; my mother is there, and I will soon come." I went to their piece of ground, for they were not going to put up their tepees that night, so I was doomed to pass another night under a wagon. As for sleep, all I got was in the day time, for I was too nervous to sleep in the night.

Next morning after our arrival at Yellow Medicine, the Indian soldiers were determined the encampment should be in a circle, and the old woman got scared and hid me again for several hours. I could not find any one who knew where Paul was. I did not know his Indian name, and they did not know him by the name of Paul. Chaska said if my boy was not brought that night he would go to Hazelwood the next morning for him, as that was where Paul formerly lived. My feet at this time were very bad; proud flesh as large as a silver dollar was eating into my foot, and the old woman said I must not walk any more for several days. Soon after she brought me out of my hiding place; she carried me to the camp. Everything was now still. She took me to her sister's tepee, who was a widow, the same person that I stayed one night with at Redwood. She prepared me a good breakfast of coffee, dried meat and potatoes and fried bread, but I could not eat, my mind was so troubled about my child. While I was sitting on the ground, drinking my coffee, a lady appeared before me whom I had known at Redwood and also at Shakopee, but had not seen her since I was in captivity before. She was feeling very badly, and complained much of her treatment, saying she had no place decent to sleep, or anything fit for a pig to eat, and begged what I had for herself and children. I pitied her very much, for many nights she said she and her children were driven out of the tepee while the medicine men were at work over a wounded man who was with them.

That afternoon, just as I had got my feet done up nicely, and Chaska had started after my boy, some one said the Indians were becoming drunk. I did not feel alarmed until Chaska drove up to the tepee very much excited; his horse was just dripping with perspiration, as if he had been out in the rain, and said a white woman had just been killed by a drunken man, and I must hide somewhere. An old squaw I had known at Yellow Medicine, called "Opa," was just in to see me, and she said she would take me up to the friendly camp of Yellow Medicine Indians, who were always encamped about one mile from us. She took Nellie on her back and we ran for some cornfields, stooping down so we could not be seen, around through potato fields, until we got out of sight of the lower camp, and at last arrived at the tepee, torn, worn, and nearly exhausted. No one knows, unless they have run for their life, how a person feels, expecting every moment to be overtaken; and when they reach a place of safety how relieved they feel. When I got to Bit-Nose's tepee, the name of Opa's husband, I felt so happy that I dropped on my knees and thanked God that he had once more brought me away from death.

I felt that night very happy. Julia Laframbois told me she had seen James that day, and he was well and happy, and old Bit-Nose prepared something for my feet that eased the pain very much.[56] Bit-Nose was Chaska's cousin, and he was a very good man. He was a farmer at Yellow Medicine, and was one of my nearest neighbors. I don't wish any one to think he was 'Cut-Nose, for that wretch was hanged, while Bit-Nose was taken care of and protected all winter by the government, and now has gone to Missouri.[57]

The morning following my arrival at Bit-Nose's tepee, Chaska drove up in a buggy and had my child with him. I did not at first recognize him, his dress was so different from when I saw him last. As I went towards him saying, "My child, my son," he was busy showing some plaything to the Indian children collected around; the little rogue manifested no joy at seeing me. I said, "James ain't you glad to see your mother." "Oh! yes, but then I had such a nice time at Paul's, I want to go back again." I tried to take him from the buggy and he said, "Do you think I am a baby, I can get out alone now." I thought he was getting very old, for he was not five until October. This night I was happy. I had my children both in my arms, and I thought I never would murmur again if I only could keep them with me. I knew my husband was alive, and I was out of reach of that villain, Hapa's clutches. I sang for the children that night; we ran around on the prairie, picked flowers, and my spirits were as light as air, although I was a prisoner. Do you who may read this think I did wrong? Many persons say I was happy with the Indians, that I did not mourn over my lot as many. Why should I mourn all the time? could I effect any good by so doing? No; instead of good I should have made trouble for myself. I tried to make myself as pleasant as I could while with my Indian friends, and in that way they learned to respect me more every day. I felt the change from civilized to savage life as much as any one, but it would do no good to keep drawing comparisons; I was there, and it was no use to borrow trouble, but try to be as contented as I could under the circumstances, but every word and action has been remembered, and turned against me to my disadvantage.

While I was at this camp Paul troubled me very much; was continually hanging around me, wanting me to go with him as his wife. One day I got a note from Mrs. Renville saying I should come with Paul and they would protect me. I sent for Miss Laframbois, and in Paul's presence and Chaska's, inquired in what way I could stay with Paul. He said as his wife, but I need not work. His Dakota wife would do the work. I asked Chaska if I should go, he said if I wished to; he did not care; he intended keeping me so as to give me up to my husband. I told Paul I would stay, for I was well treated by Chaska, for he had never asked me to be his wife, and it was wrong in him to ask such a thing, being a Christian.

After remaining at this camp two days, Opa said I had better return, as Paul was determined to have me for his wife, and if I went back to Chaska's tepee I would be more safe than with them. She sent for him to come, but as it drew near night, and he came not, she took Nellie and we started back. We met him, and we all got in and rode back to his aunt's. James was much disturbed to think he should be out that day, as it was raining, for he was very well dressed in his new Indian costume, made for him by Paul's wife, and he was afraid of his soiling it. I went to Chaska's aunt's and he said I must stay there until his mother made her a tepee, and I must help her. Chaska had lived in a house previous to the outbreak, was a good farmer, and worked hard. When forced to leave his house he was obliged to go with his sister and her husband, as they had no tepee. His wife had been dead but a few months and he was still wearing mourning for her. I remained with his aunt, assisting his mother to make our tepee, sitting out in the hot sun sewing, the white cloth drawing more heat towards us. I was afraid my eyes would be injured, but I see no change in my person only the color. I do not think I will ever recover from the sunburn.

Just before the battle of Birch Coolie, Chaska said he was going to the Big Woods to drive up cattle, and I had better go back to Bit-Nose's again, and said his mother would go with me.[58]

I saw Mrs. Decamp again this day; her tepee was near ours.[59] She was very unhappy, and begged me to ask her people to give her a squaw dress, as I could speak Dakota.[60] She was very filthy, and so were her children. She came in one morning and said she was nearly starved, and I gave her all I had left from my breakfast. She sat a long time talking about our situation. She remarked several times during our conversation, that she would be thankful if she was as comfortable as I was. I told her she took a wrong course with the Indians; that she cried and fretted all the while, making them feel cross towards her; that they gave her the best they had, and she must try and be patient; that her life would be in danger if she kept on complaining and threatening them; it done no good, only enraged them towards her. One day after a battle she heard all the Indians were killed. She felt very glad, as we all did; but I, for one, tried to restrain my feelings. Not her; she exclaimed, "Oh! that is good: I wish every one dead; I would like to cut their throats," taking up a knife and flourishing it. This was very unwise, for many Indians understand every word that is said in our language; and one stood near her, and made this remark in Dakota, "You die for that talk." Soon after she went up to a half-breed's about one mile away. He had sent a girl for her, knowing what the Indians had threatened. Soon she disappeared entirely, and we all thought she had been secretly murdered, for the Indians disliked her very much. Chaska often told me to tell her not to come into our tepee, saying that the Indians would learn to dislike me too. But she made her escape and reached Fort Ridgely soon after the death of her husband. Poor woman, I feel very much for her, although she misrepresented many things. But I know she was about crazy while in camp; and then, the death of her husband must have affected her very much. I well remember her saying to me, "Mrs. Wakefield, your husband is really dead. I heard an Indian say he had seen his body." At that time I was in hopes he was alive, and her words seemed to paralyze me. When I could speak, I made this remark, "If that is so, I might as well pass the remainder of my days here as any place. He was my all, I care not to live; life will be a burden to me." This had been told in a very different way. Another time she was speaking of our situation, and she said she could not imagine anything worse than our being in that camp. I said, "Don't say so, Mrs. Decamp there are many worse things than this. She said no; she thought it worse than 'Torment.'" I told her that I had, in my life, passed through trials that were worse to bear, for I could see no hope, no bright place in the future; that now I could, for I knew that sometime we would be rescued; that we were well treated, and we might be abused; that we were comfortably fed and lodged when we might be left on the plains to starve. I tried every way to encourage the lady, but she was determined to look at the worst, and would not be comforted. But her *situation* at the time had much to do with her feelings, so I will not blame her. My disposition is always to feel that God sends our trials, and I must bear them as well as I can, trusting him to "deliver us from all evils."

I went to Bit-Nose's again, but cannot remember how long I remained there, but it was after the battle of Birch Coolie, for the next morning after that fight I removed with their family farther up the country with sad feelings. I gazed on my home, as it was enveloped in flames the morning we started. I had very little hopes of ever seeing that place again, for the Indians said they were going to the Red River now without stopping again, and I thought I should surely die before reaching there. Chaska had always said the soldiers will soon come and you will be rescued; and he promised me if they came not before the river began to freeze, he would try to take me down in a canoe; but said I had better wait for the soldiers, for if we were discovered by the Indians we would all be killed. I tried to keep up good courage, but it was with a sad heart I drove myself and children over the prairie that day. I have driven many horses, but none ever compared with the one I drove that day. He was an Indian pony, and I should judge, had a good deal of the mule about him, for he would go just contrary to the lines. I was amused but at the same time I was vexed, and I often think of the picture we made. I was kept constantly busy trying to keep all things straight; the back part of our wagon was piled high above our heads with goods and under our feet; and the seat of our wagon was what had been our pantry. My feet were astride a jar of lard, melted like oil; a crock with molasses, a pan of flour, with bread, vegetables, dishes, all mixed up together. Now it was quite an undertaking to keep all things in order—pony, two children and pantry.

We got along very well, considering all things, until I got to a creek, when the pony, not having had water that morning, became much excited for a drink, and plunged forward regardless of his precious freight; but he did not go far, for he was soon fast in the mud. I unloaded my passengers with help, and gave a jump, thinking I should reach a nice piece of grass; but when I struck I was fast to my knees in a patch of boggy ground. How I was to extricate myself I knew not; but I laughed at the thought of my predicament. At last the children began calling, "Mamma, what are you doing down in the mud?" I found that I could not get out without help, and called to Bit-Nose's girl to come to my assistance. She brought a board and I got out; but what a sight was I! completely covered with mud in my struggles to free myself.

Pony, as soon as released of his load, rushed into the water, got a drink, hurried himself up the bank, regardless of our provisions. My blanket was considerably soiled, but everything was otherwise safe. We rode the rest of the way quietly, but my boy would occasionally say, "Mamma, why don't you turn round and drive to Shakopee?" I said, "Why, you know the Indians will not let us." "Oh, dear me! mamma, what do you suppose God made Indians for? I wish they were all dead, don't you mamma?"

We camped about three miles west of Hazelwood, but it was a long time, as usual, before they could decide upon the best place. This day I was treated to bread and molasses: the children thinking it a treat. As we sat eating it, under the wagon, on a piece of carpet which they always provided me with, I heard a voice in my own language, and Miss E. B—— came towards me.[61] Glad was I to see her. I knew she was a prisoner, but had not caught a glimpse of her since I had been in captivity. She looked finely in her squaw dress, but did not compliment me very highly on my looks. She said she would not have known me if she had met me on the prairie, for I was so much changed. My hair turned as white as an old woman's with fright the night I was taken prisoner.

After being at Bit-Nose's some days, I got nervous, and wished to go to the old woman's, for the Yellow Medicine Indians were expecting to be attacked by the Lower Indians, because they would not come and join them in their camp.

Opa said she would like me to stay, but told me I would be more safe if I was back with Chaska, so they sent for him. He disliked to have me leave Bit-Nose's, because if we traveled I could ride, if I was with them, and if with him I must walk, as they had but one horse now, he and Hapa had separated, but all I thought of was life. I preferred to go back even if I had to walk, rather than stay, expecting death every minute as I did. Chaska and his cousin Dowonca came for me: one took Nellie, the other James, on their horses, and I followed by their side.

Little Crow's camp had not crossed the creek, therefore it was three miles from the Yellow Medicine camp. When we were going along I could see Mr. Riggs's church and house all in flames.

I think I suffered in my mind more at Yellow Medicine and that neighborhood, than at any other spot, as it recalled so many pleasant scenes past and gone; it spoke so forcibly of home, husband, children, all united; now where were we, and what would be our fate? Would we ever be together again?

I got back to Chaska's tepee, and it seemed good to get back, for everything was so clean, new and sweet. I was nearly devoured with fleas at Bit-Nose's, for they had thirteen dogs. About this time my baby became quite sick, and I thought for many days she would die. I was told that in Dr. Williamson's house, which was as yet unburnt, I would find medicine. I asked Chaska to take me there, as it was several miles, and I dared not go alone. One day he took James, his cousin and myself, and we visited the house, where I often went while at home. What a change! Their once happy home was all destroyed. It looked as if an earthquake had done its worst work, for everything was broken up and mixed together. Bedsteads, stoves, book and medicines. I could not keep from shrieking as I thought of the old people that had passed all their lives among these same people, and now how they were repaid! They had been compelled to flee, forsaking all, after passing nearly all their lives among these Indians. They had a delightful home with many of the comforts of eastern farmers around them. Oh! how my heart ached as I passed through the rooms where I had so often seen their friendly faces. Now where were they? Turned out into the world to seek a home in their old age; and why, I asked myself, have these Indians lived quietly so long, and never, until this late day, done any wrong towards the whites? I could not think of any other cause than this—it may be right, it may be wrong; but such is my belief—: That our own people, not the Indians were to blame. Had they not, for years, been suffering? Had they not been cheated unmercifully, and now their money had been delayed; no troops were left to protect the frontier and their Agent, their "father," had left them without money, food or clothing, and gone off to the war. I often said to the Indians that if they had let innocent people alone, and robbed us all they would never have been blamed. But they knew no justice but in dealing out death for their wrongs.

I sat down on the door-step and cried while taking a view of my situation now and what it was only two weeks before. At last my boy said, "Don't cry, mamma, you know we shall get away soon," and for his sake I dried my tears and endeavored to put on a cheerful face.

The bell from the top of the building was being rung furiously by some boys; the Indians were tearing, crushing everything with their reach. I went into the garden and gathered a few tomatoes, and came away feeling sad, very sad.

While at this camp I suffered very much bringing water, as the bank was almost perpendicular; all the way I could get up would be by catching a twig with one hand, and pull myself up, and then catch another. Many times a twig would break, and down I would go, feet foremost, to the bottom, deluged by the water I was carrying. One day I went for water, and as my feet were dirty, I tho't I would wash them; as the pail was an old one I thought I would wash my feet in it, for I could reach the water only by lying down on my face; so I thought I would dip it up and wash, and then wash the pail. When I got back to the tepee the family were all in great commotion. Chaska brought in an interpreter, who said I had committed a great sin by putting my feet in the pail, for all vessels belonging to a tepee are sacred, and no women are allowed to put their feet in them or step over them.[62] I told him I could scrub the pail, but he said it would not do, for they would never use it again, and they did not. It was turned upside down, and when we removed they left it on the prairie.

Speaking of their superstitions, reminds me of many things that were interesting to me, and I will relate them here. Their war spears and medicine bags are sacred things; a female is never allowed to touch them.[63] By day they are tied to a pole in front of the tepee; at night they are brought in and tied high above the head of the chief man in the tepee. One morning I noticed they were about to fall down and was going towards them to fasten them up, when the old woman said, "Stop, stop, white woman, stop, I will call some man." She appeared much frightened, and ran in a great hurry and brought in a boy. When the men go to battle they always take their spears with them, thinking a few painted sticks will assist them in their undertaking.

I offended many an Indian God by stepping over axes, pipes, or persons' feet, or some such silly thing. They never wash their hands in any dish; they fill their mouths and then spit it out on to their hands. I could not do this way, so they begged me a wash dish from some half-breeds.

I don't remember what time in the month we started for Red Iron's village, but I have not forgotten what I suffered that day, for I had to walk all the distance, which was sixteen miles.[64] My mare that Chaska had, was this day, for the first time, hitched to the poles, Indian fashion. Poor animal, I felt bad for her, as she had been made a great pet of by myself and husband. When the poles were first fastened on and, she took a few steps, she began prancing, which threw everything in all directions. As soon as she got quiet they put James on her back, and I with Nellie on mine, the old woman leading the horse, we commenced our march towards Lac qui Parle; we walked without resting even for a drink of water, for sixteen miles.[65] They seemed to feel very bad because they could not give me a ride, but it was no use to mourn; everyone had a load without taking me, and so I plodded on. Sometimes as Nellie would fall asleep the old woman would tie her on to the bundle which was fastened to the poles, and she would ride until a sudden jolt would awaken her, then I would have to quiet her and would be forced to walk as fast the horse to keep her quiet. The sun is very powerful on these prairies, and the dust was stifling, and the perspiration and dust did not add to my looks. I would hear the Indians say, "White woman got a dirty face," but had no idea how I looked until I went to the river (my looking glass) to arrange my dress. The last few miles we traveled that day I experienced more pain than I ever did in my life before. I might have been tracked by the blood that ran from my feet and legs, cut by the tall, dry grass. We could not go in the road, but right on the prairie, the carriages filling the road. Glad was I when we made a stop, and I told Chaska that I could certainly die if I had to walk any further. He said he was sorry, but he wanted me to stay at Bit-Nose's so I could ride, but I would not, and all he could do he had done, and he said I had better go back now, but I preferred to remain with his family to going back and being killed by Little Crow.

We remained at Red Iron's village some little time while their letters were carried to Fort Ridgely, from Little Crow to H. H. Sibley. One morning Tom Robertson and another man, a half-breed, went with letters; soon after the Indian soldiers left, crossed the river, and all in our neighborhood believed they had gone to intercept and murder them.[66] There was great alarm, for the Indians said if they killed them they would return and kill all the rest of the half-breeds and prisoners. When I heard this I dropped as one struck with apoplexy; I could not speak for awhile, my teeth chattered and I shivered with fear. I then thought of what Chaska had many times told me, that if I was in danger, to tell the Indians I was his wife, and I would be saved. So I said to an Indian, "I am Chaska's wife, will they kill me." He said, "No," but he believed I was telling an untruth. I went back to the old woman's and told Chaska. He said I done very wrong in saying so, for there was no truth in the story. But I did not consider how it would sound. I would have called myself the evil spirit's wife if I thought by so doing I could save my life. I suppose many Indians really thought I was his wife, for there was such an excitement all the time I forgot all about contradicting it. One day before this a half-breed woman came in and Mrs. Decamp with her. They said Little Crow was going to destroy all the whites, but would spare all who had Indian blood in them. I made up this story, which I will relate here. I said I was safe, as I was part Indian. I knew the lady had known me in Shakopee many years, and she did not believe me. I said I was about an eighth-breed; that my grandfather married a squaw many years ago in the west, and took her east, and I was one of her descendants; that I had some pride about acknowledging it, but now perhaps it would save my life. I then asked her if she did remember how very dark my mother was, then she became convinced. I was sure this half-breed woman would tell it all around, and I would be spared. I know it was wrong to tell such falsehoods, but I felt as if my God knew my thoughts and He would pardon me for doing as I did. Now to this day that woman believes me part Indian, because I never had an opportunity to contradict it.

While we were camped at Ma a ha's, or Red Iron's, the camp was quiet; soldiers would go off in scouting parties, but the majority of the Indians were around playing cards, shooting at ducks, &c.[67] The old women were busy drying corn and potatoes, cutting and drying beef, laying in a stock for winter. I assisted at all these operations willingly, for I thought I might save my children from starvation on those plains, where we were bound, for I had given up all hopes of being rescued by Sibley.

I had not many idle moments. I made short gowns for squaws, made bread, fried meat and potatoes, brought water, and went to the river three or four times a day to wash my baby's clothing, for her diarrhea was growing worse daily.

It was quite amusing to see us white women at the river washing. The banks for several miles usually were lined with Indians with their horses and cattle, boys and squaws swimming, causing it to be very muddy, so we would go out up to our waists to get a clear drink or a place to wash. When we finished we would come out and shake ourselves like dogs and go back to our tepees with our wet bundles on our backs, I have slept many a night in my wet clothes, and never took cold while I was there.

The Indians were all very kind to me; they brought me books and papers to read, and I would make them shirts, so as to return their favors. Many times when I have been coming up the steep bank of the river, all out of breath, bringing water, some Indian would take my pails out of my hands and carry them for me. Now this for a white man would not be considered much, but for an Indian it is a great thing, for they never bring wood or water. Every little act like that I remember, and let who blame me that may, I shall say there are many, very many good, kind hearted Indians. One day I was down by the river waiting to get a chance to fill my pails, when I saw an Indian approaching. I was standing near a tree resting my head against it. He came very near and spoke to me in English, "Mrs. Wakefield, this makes me feel very bad." I then recognized him: it was a Christian Indian called "Comoska," who had been at my house. His wife worked for me all one winter and he knew I was suffering very much carrying water. He got off his horse, shook hands and burst forth crying. I sat down on the ground and cried for near an hour, while this man, Indian as he was, gave me such advice as would have astonished persons. He said I must put my trust in God; never forget that he had power to save, and feel as if his eye was upon me, his arms around me, and all would be well. He said he would do all he could for me, and he had often prayed for me. Now this was an evidence of God's love, for he stood firm in His truth although surrounded by savage and heathen Indians, trying to have him forsake the white man's God and return to the worship of sticks and stones.[68]

In the nights, while at Red Iron's we had a good chance to sleep, for the young men had great dances and councils, so it left the old women and myself time to rest. Before that time hardly a night passed without our cooking all night, as they would have a tepee full of company playing cards and singing. The old women would fill the kettles with beef and potatoes as soon as it was dark, pound their coffee and commence frying their bread. The company would soon assemble; they would generally commence eating as soon as they came in, each one bringing his own dish or "wooden trencher." Then they would smoke, (I must take a whiff with them, or they would be offended) then they would play cards, for they are inveterate gamblers, often losing all they had in the world, taking off shirt, blanket and moccasins, and going home entirely naked except their "breech-clout." After playing many would lie down and commence pounding their breasts as a drum, all the while singing, "Hi! Hi!" with some thing about the "Isan Tonkas," or white men, (meaning Big Knives, as they call the whites from their wearing swords when they first came among them.) They would sing, shout and pound their breasts, when up would jump one, then another and then the "Wacipa," or dance, would commence; keeping constantly on the move, one foot shuffling before the other, until they were completely exhausted, when, one by one, they would fall back and go to sleep, after which it would be quiet.[69] Soon, however, one would awaken and then another; the kettles would be re-filled and the programme would be repeated, and this would be kept up until day began to dawn.

After leaving Red Iron's village there was no rest, either night or day, for they knew when the soldiers left the Fort, and they expected they would come right on. Many a time I have run for the woods with the squaws thinking the soldiers were very near, and they said Sibley was going to shell the camp.

Every night now, the old women kept watch keeping the door open so as to watch their horses, for we were drawing near the Sisseton country, and Standing Buffalo had threatened to take all their horses and cattle, if they came up where he was.[70]

I should have suffered with the cold at this time if Chaska and his mother had not been so kind as to lend me their blankets to cover me, and they would draw around the fire to keep warm. Where could you find white people that would do like that? Go without to cover others. Was this kindness or not, let me ask you?

The Indians made much sport of the slow movements of Sibley; said the white people did not care much about their wives and children or they would have hurried on faster.

Many nights the old crier would go around, saying the soldiers are coming, make ready for battle. Sometimes he would say the white women are to be killed in the morning; and our feelings were dreadful living in that way. Then when morning came they would tell a different story. Little Crow had a plan like this; when the soldiers came he was going to send us out in our squaw dresses, thereby causing the white men to kill those they came to rescue. I had no fears of anything of this kind. When Standing Buffalo came, Chaska was very nervous. The lower Indians are very much afraid of the Sissetons, and they thought he would kill the white women, but he came and shook hands with some of us, and said that, if the Indians brought us up into his country, he would take us and bring us back to our friends.

When the news came that Sibley was near Yellow Medicine, and that the Indians were going down to fight him, I felt very uneasy, for Chaska said he and his cousins were going, and I would be left without any protection. He and many others went, and I passed a wretched day. We heard all kinds of reports about the friendly Indian camp, that Little Crow had threatened before leaving. About nine o'clock in the evening, Chaska returned, saying that Little Crow was a bad man, and he would not go out again unless he was forced to. He remained at home two days, when it seemed as if the squaws were crazy; they would move their tepees every few hours, sometimes on the prairie, then into the timber.

One morning a messenger came, saying that every man that could carry a gun should come down immediately, or he would shoot all that refused. I tried to urged Chaska not to go, but he said Little Crow would say I had prevented him, and that he would destroy us both. The morning he left he seemed very anxious to impress upon my mind the necessity of remaining with his mother. Several times he came in and said, "You stay where you are; don't go up to the friendly camp; don't you talk to any half-breed or white women, if you do you will be killed." I knew these friendly Indians were trying to get the prisoners, now they knew Sibley was coming, and I thought he was fearful I would go off, as some had done. After he had been gone sometime, his cousin, a half-breed told me that Little Crow intended to destroy the friendly camp as soon as he returned; therefore Chaska's anxiety to have me stay where I was.

I stayed with his mother as I promised, although all left but two other Americans besides myself. If Little Crow had been victorious, all would have been killed; but God ordered otherwise, and they were all saved.

Chaska was gone two days and one night. When he returned, I inquired how the battle had gone; he said they had killed one hundred and fifty white men, and only lost two Indians. I felt as if all hope was now gone, and could not help saying that I believed the Lord was on their side. But night told different stories, and I should have known it from the mourning and crying from the many tepees, if they had not told me. Any one that has heard one squaw lament can judge of the noise of four or five hundred all crying at once. As soon as it was dark Chaska advised me to lie down so my shadow would not show on the tepee cloth, as he was afraid they would shoot through and kill me, they were so excited. They held a council that night, and decided to give us up, and I was told that a letter would be sent to Sibley the next morning, requesting him to come for us in the morning. They had many plans. They did not get breakfast—only roasted potatoes in the ashes, and commenced packing up preparing for a start. I asked if they were not going to give us up; they said five half-breeds would take us down to Sibley's camp. I then said I would not go, for I knew we would all be killed by Little Crow's soldiers. I told them I had rather remain with them and wait until Sibley came. Soon the camp began to break up, and the old woman gave me some potatoes, saying that I must eat them, as upon the plains where we were going, we could get no more. I threw myself down, crying, on the ground. Chaska said, "What are you crying about?" I said, "I do not want to go away with the Indians." He said, "You did not wish to go with the half-breeds; what will you do? The Indians are all going very soon." I told him I thought the Indians were going to wait for Sibley, and try to make peace. He said they were afraid to stay for fear they would all be killed, and were going on, leaving us with the half-breeds. Soon after this conversation, two chiefs came in, saying that Joe Campbell was going for Other Day, the Indian who rescued the people from death at Yellow Medicine. In the meantime they wished me to write an account of my treatment by Chaska, and the other Indians I had been acquainted with. I told them it was very foolish for me to write, for I could tell the people just as well as to write, and I began to be suspicious of some evil. I was afraid they would murder us and hide our bodies, and carry our notes to the Fort. I wrote the note, however, but was determined I would not go without more protection than five men over that prairie.

Soon after writing the note, I was told to hurry and change my dress for one of my own, as the soldiers were coming, and it would be wrong for them to see me in a squaw dress. I dressed in a great hurry. I could not tell what was to be done, there were so many stories. At last we were ready, and we left our tepee and my Indian friends, who had given me a home and protected me for six weeks. The old woman shook hands and kissed me, and said, "You are going back where you will have good, warm houses and plenty to eat, and we will starve on the plains this winter. O, that 'bad man,' who has caused so much trouble," meaning Little Crow. They cried over James, and begged me to leave him with them. He was a great favorite with the Indians all the time I was with them. Chaska led Mr. Gleason's dog. Dowonca carried James, and I with Nellie, we started for the Indian soldiers' camp. A large American flag was flying and we sat ourselves down on the grass beneath its folds, awaiting the decision of our captors relative to our going or staying. All seemed anxious to have us go, still none wished to go below, but a few half-breeds. At last they said they would carry us down; then I began to act like one crazy. I declared I would not go; whereupon Mr. Campbell said I could go and stay with his wife, who was a white woman, until his return, as the friendly Indians were going to stay where they were. We stayed on this hill until Little Crow's camp had gone, then we went over to the friendly camp, Chaska and his mother bidding me goodbye, and leaving.

I went to Mrs. Renville's tepee.[71] Her husband is a half-breed. She was like a wild woman. She was afraid to speak, fearing she might be heard by Indian spies. There were about sixty tepees left in the morning after the others had gone. Instead of taking us below, the Indians left us and went on horseback carrying letters to Sibley, hurrying him on—telling him how we were situated—that we were liable to be attacked at any moment by Little Crow's soldiers. I had not been in Mrs. Renville's tepee more than an hour, when her husband came in saying many Indians were returning and were anxious to camp with us. Among them was Chaska and all his family. Soon Eagle Head appeared, and said I had better come back to Chaska's tepee; that they had decided to remain, and would feel more safe if I was with them when Sibley came. He also said if Little Crow returned, as they expected he would at night, I would be more safe with them than with the half-breeds; so I decided to go, as his tepee was not more than three rods from Mrs. Renville's.[72] She was quite angry because I left, and said I must be crazy for he would kill me. I told her they had protected me for six weeks, and I was not afraid of their injuring me now. But I knew her object in having me stay, for she said that Maz-coota-Meni had no prisoner to give up to Sibley, and she wished me to go to his tepee, so he could have the credit of releasing me. [73] I felt if I could be of service to any one, I would rather benefit those who had taken care of me when I was in danger, than to favor strange Indians. I many times sent for this lady, when I was a prisoner, but she dared not come, so she knew not of their kindness to me.

Among those that decided to remain were Wabasha, Wacota, and parts of several bands. [74]

The half-breeds returned from Sibley's camp early in the after noon. [75] We looked for the soldiers all night, but they came not. There was no sleep. Every man was on guard. Entrenchments were dug around our tepees and pits within, for we expected we would be attacked before morning, as Little Crow's brother had remained around as a spy, and surely would notify Little Crow of the non-appearance of our soldiers.

We passed a very anxious night. Morning came, but no soldiers were visible. "What can be the matter?" was the cry. Some Indians came in, saying they had returned because their force was not large enough. Chaska became frightened, and said he thought I had better go to some half-breeds, and take his mother with me, and he would go off. Miss E. B—— and I persuaded him to remain, promising him our protection. He said he felt as if they would kill all the Indians; but we told him if Sibley had promised to shake hands with all that remained and gave up their prisoners, he would do as he said. At last he decided to stay, saying, "If I am killed, I will blame you for it." Now I will always feel that I am responsible for that man's murder, and will reproach myself for urging him to remain.

How we looked for Sibley all the next day, but he did not come; all that night we watched also, but no signs of him yet. Where can he be? he was only twenty-five miles away. We at last concluded he was afraid. The Indians began to get uneasy, and said "Little Crow will be back and kill us, if Sibley does not soon come." How we blamed him for making us suffer as we did, for we expected death every instant. The second night we waited for him, an Indian came in saying they had only traveled eight miles, and it was now thirty-six hours since he got our message, and they had camped for the night, spending hours to entrench themselves. An army of over two thousand leaving us, a little handful of persons, with only about one hundred men to protect us! The time taken to entrench themselves, passed in marching, would have brought them to our relief; but God watched over us, and kept those savages back. To him I give all the honor and glory; Sibley I do not even thank, for he deserved it not.

The second night of our stay, Dowonca had a religious performance in our tepee. The females were excluded. They were trying to ascertain by their conjuring if the soldiers would hurt them.

That night every Indian was on guard, the report reaching us that Little Crow was advancing towards us for battle. There were no more midnight councils and dances; all was still and quiet except the medicine men at the performances over the sick. The Indians believe when a person is sick they are possessed with evil spirits, and these conjurers stand over them and rattle gourds, thinking by so doing they will drive out the evil spirits; and when some are about leaving, the squaws rush at the imaginary beings and pretend to shoot them, or stab them with their knives, all the time singing, talking, imploring their gods to help them. It is enough to make a well person sick. I was one day in a tepee where an Indian woman was in labour; she had been suffering many hours, and these conjurers were at work rattling and singing. Her husband soon came in, and began cutting out little images of stained hide. I was told that he would stand at the door of the tepee, and, as occasion required, throw one at her, expecting this would assist nature in bring forth the child.

Poor superstitious beings, how much they are to be pitied! Very few of them believe in any God besides a painted stone or stick; ought we to expect these creatures to act with reason and judgment like ourselves?

Just for one moment, think of all they have borne for years, and you will wonder, as I do, that they saved as many lives as they did, for their religion teaches them that evil for evil, good for good, is right. Many ask me why they killed so many that had befriended them. I myself asked that question many times while I was with them, and I will give one answer that was given me.

An Indian, having plenty of ducks, went one day to Beaver Creek and wished to exchange them for potatoes. He said, when telling me of it, that his ducks were fresh and good; that they took them and gave him potatoes that a hog could not eat, they were so soft. Now, this is the way many befriended the Indians; gave them what they could not eat themselves. This is the way the Indians have been treated for years. I know the Indians have butchered the whites, and I wish every guilty one punished: but I cannot blame them as many do, for I am sure they had cause, and very strong reasons for being revenged on some persons who have been living off their lands and money, while they were starving. If these Indians had commenced this outbreak out of pure wickedness, I would feel as many do—that they ought to be exterminated; but it is not so; they took the only way they knew of getting restitution and we all want that when we are wronged.

I have many very firm friends in the Indian camp, and I feel for them as much pity and sorrow as if they were white; for I have sat and listened to their tales of suffering and distress until my heart bled for them. I pray God they may for the future be more mercifully dealt with by those that are in authority over them.

To return to my narrative: the night passed without an attack, as anticipated; but we could hear no tidings of the soldiers, and we really thought they had returned. Sibley had requested us to remain where we were, or we should have gone down. That was the message brought back by the half-breeds. Now it was the third day, and we were getting very impatient, but not as much so as our Indians friends, who often said, "We will go on; there is no use waiting longer." About noon of the third day we saw them coming, and then, instead of joy, I felt feelings of anger enter my breast, as I saw such an army, for I felt that part at least might have come to our rescue before that late hour. While they were coming up we saw a party of Indians near us, and several half breeds and Indians started for them, and found them to be a party of Sissetons who had come up just in advance of the soldiers, bringing with them three prisoners—one girl and two boys. Joe Campbell demanded the children, but they refused to give them up, and said they were going to kill them; but Joe made a sudden spring and secured the girl, while the Indians saved the boys, when the Sissetons fled.[76] I conversed with the girl; she said they were near the soldiers for a long time, so she could hear their voices; that they crawled on their knees much of the time, to avoid being seen. Her feet were all blisters, but the boys the Indians carried part of the way. It seems very strange they should spare so many helpless children and murder their parents, when they are such a trouble to them. I have seen squaws carry white children nine and ten years old on their backs, and let their own walk. Now this was out of real good feeling, for they certainly had no selfish motives in so doing, and the world does the Indian great injustice when they say they *saved persons only for selfish purposes.*

As Sibley's forces drew near, the Indians became much alarmed, and drew within their tepees. We were all eager to get to them immediately, but we were told we should remain where we were until Sibley came over. The soldiers encamped about a quarter of a mile from our camp. Sibley sent a messenger, saying he would come over after dinner and talk with the Indians.

About this time some squaws brought me a dress belonging to Mrs. Dr. Humphrey.[77] How strange are God's ways! How little did I think when I assisted her in making this dress of my ever wearing it, and at such a place and under such circumstances. Now she was dead, and I, where was I? In a camp of Indians, not knowing but I should be, at last, murdered by them, for I had many miles to travel before reaching civilization.

It may be well to speak of this family here. It was with them, you will remember, that I passed one week previous to my captivity. On the first day of the outbreak, Dr. Humphrey and wife, with three children, fled, crossed the Minnesota River, ascended the high hills and entered a house for a drink of water. The family had all left. Johnny, aged twelve went to the spring for water, and on returning, heard a shot and saw his father fall dead before the door. He said his mother closed the door and fastened it. The Indians tried to get in, but finding it secured, fired the building, and she and her two beautiful children perished in the flames. The boy secreted himself and made his escape. When near Fort Ridgely he met the soldiers, returned with them, and was in that fatal fight at the Ferry. Still he was unhurt, and with the remnant of that brave band reach Fort Ridgely an orphan, homeless, but not friendless, for God was with him and raised up kind friends for him.

My dinner was eaten for the last time with my Indian friends; they were very sad, seeming to be dreading some evil. About three o'clock Sibley and staff arrived, and after conversing a few minutes with the Indians, ordered those having prisoners to bring them forward and give them up. Old Eagle Head and Chaska came for me: before leaving the old woman tore her shawl and gave me half, as I had none.

Chaska trembled with fear. He said, "You are a good woman, you must talk good to your white people or they will kill me; you know I am a good man, and did not shoot Mr. Gleason, and I saved your life. If I had been a bad man I would have gone with those bad chiefs." I assured him he need not fear, they would not injure him; but how vain were all my promises; poor man, he found the whites deceitful, even unto his death.

After I was introduced to Sibley, Mr. Riggs, and others, they requested me to point out the Indian who had saved me. He came forward as I called his name; and when I told them how kind he had been they shook hands with him, and made quite a hero of him for a short time. I was compelled to leave the circle about this time, on account of my baby, and went to a tepee near, and while there the company broke up, taking the white women with them; two or three officers remained to escort me over. When I got to the camp I found the soldiers in a state of great excitement, and all were eager to catch a glimpse of us. I was conducted to a large tent and soon it was surrounded with soldiers.

We nearly suffocated for want of air. The tent I was in contained twenty-four persons. We suffered much for want of bedding, for there was no provision made for us, although they were so many weeks preparing for a start to rescue us. My children took very bad colds, and I wished many times I had a tepee to sleep in. Now I wish to be distinctly understood in this remark: I did not wish myself back in a tepee, I only wanted the comforts of one, for I was a vast deal more comfortable with the Indians in every respect than I was during my stay in that soldiers camp, and was treated more respectfully by those savages than I was by those in that camp, when we were given some straw to lie on, and a blanket for each. We had to cook our own food, exposed to the gaze of several hundred ignorant men, that would surround our fires as soon as we commenced cooking, so we could not breathe for want of air. I have many times been forced to go to some officer and request a guard around us, so we could cook without molestation. With the Indians my life was very different; the old squaws doing all the cooking, unless I took a fancy to assist.

The nights had got to be very cold now, and our tent was constructed for a stove, but we had none. Sometimes we would make a fire on the ground, and we would be forced to lie down on our faces, the smoke was so dense.

My clothing consisted of a thin gingham dress, one cotton skirt, no under garments of any kind. I had a pair of moccasins, but no stockings of any kind, and half of a shawl. I am a large woman, and the squaws could not find any that would be large enough. I weighed, three days before the outbreak, two hundred and three pounds. When I got to Shakopee, eight weeks after, I weighed one hundred and sixty-three pounds. My travels and anxiety had worn upon me so much.

The first evening I passed at Camp Release was a very pleasant one.[78] We were serenaded, and all the dainties of the camp were brought to us. I think the soldiers must have thought we had fasted for many weeks, to judge by the quantity brought to us. My children never knew what it was to be hungry in the Indian camp, for food was plenty, and that which was good. Nearly every day some little dainty was brought to "Pajute Wicaste Tawicu"—English doctor's wife. I really thought my children would be made sick by the Indians, for they were continually feeding them.

I will here say, that the family I was with were not the greasy, lousy, filthy Indians, we used to see around begging. There is a great difference in them, and a person visiting the Agencies would have been astonished to see the hard working men and women, but clean and neat as our own farmers. I have employed squaws in my family that were educated by the missionaries, that could read and write in their own language, and could make coats, pants, or shirts far better than many a white girl of the present generation. Such are some of the good works of the missionaries.

I always had in our tepee, a towel, soap, and wash dish, and I never knew of any of the family to neglect washing and combing before eating. I had my own corner of the tepee, and was not allowed to go over to the other part, and they never came near mine.

They are foolishly particular about some things. The fire is in the centre of the tepee, and I never was allowed to pass around the fire. I must go out on my own side, for I would be going into my neighbor's domain, if I went across. I used to get very tired sitting in one place with my baby. My little boy, however, enjoyed his life while there, for I could raise the tepee cloth and watch him; and he would play for hours on the grass, with the Indian boys.

I often asked him if he would not like to see his father, and he would answer, very indifferently, "Yes, but I wish he would come here, I would like to stay if he would."

The morning after my arrival at Camp Release I went over to the Indians' camp for some articles I left, in company with a woman who was taken near Hutchinson.[79] She was taken captive by an Indian who had a wife, and this woman caused great trouble in their tepee. She declared to me she was not his wife, but said she slept on the same pillow and was covered with his blanket. But his wife got very jealous, and one day threw a knife at her husband, inflicting a severe wound. He was very angry, and Mrs. A——s a was obliged to go over to the friendly camp for protection.[80]

We attended, while there, a Dakota prayer meeting. Chaska was much frightened. He called me to the door, and said they had arrested two Indians, and if he was arrested he would know I had told falsehoods about him, and then he would lie too.

I told him I had a long conversation with one of the officers, and he said that he should be pardoned on account of his kindness to me and my children. He appeared much pleased, and I went back to Camp Release. In the afternoon they had a sort of court of inquiry, and we were all questioned by Col. Crooks and Marshall, J. V. D. Hurd, S. R. Riggs, and others.[81] I was the first one questioned. I related to them briefly what I have here written, after which, Col. Marshall said, "If you have anything more of a private nature to relate, you can communicate it to Mr. Riggs." I did not understand until he explained himself more fully. I told them it was just as I related, it was all. They thought it very strange I had no complaints to make, but did not appear to believe me. I was then told I might go, and not wishing to walk a quarter of a mile alone, I went to a tepee near by occupied by Miss La Flambois. While there I sent for Chaska. He was looking very pale and frightened. He said the white men were not doing as they promised and he knew they would kill him. I endeavored to persuade him to leave, promising to take care of his mother. He said, "No; I am not a coward, I am not afraid to die. All I care about is my poor old mother, she will be left alone." He said he was sorry I persuaded him to remain; that his mother was very angry with me for not letting him go. I still held out strong hopes to him, insisting that he should be spared. Soon after I left he was arrested. I was not much concerned at first, for I supposed he would soon be liberated, unless they could find something more against him than I knew of. That evening many of the officers were in, laughing and talking. We were all acting like little children let loose from school, not really sensible of what we were saying, when some one remarked, "We have seven of those Indians fast." When Capt. Grant said, "Yes; we have seven of the black devils, and before to-morrow night they will hang as high as Haman."[82] I asked if they had him who had protected me. He said, "Yes; and he will swing with the rest." Then I made this remark, "Capt. Grant, if you hang that man, I will shoot you, if it is not in twenty years." Then thinking how it sounded, I said, "But you must first teach me to shoot, for I am afraid of a gun, unloaded even." Now this remark has been reported through the State. Any one well acquainted with me knows my violent impulsive disposition, and would not heed what I say when I am excited, for I very often say to my children, when I am out of patience, "Do be quiet, or I will whip you to death." Now I never meant to do one any more than I did the other; it is a rude way I have of expressing myself.

The first man tried was the negro and several days were passed in bringing in testimony, when every one knew he was guilty.[83] But it gave Little Crow a good chance to escape, thereby prolonging this war; for Little Crow was only six miles away when Sibley arrived. Now arises a thought—an inquiry: If Sibley had not found us waiting on that prairie for him, would he have returned or would he have gone farther? If he intended to go farther, why did he stop where he did? for he was sure of the Indians who had been waiting two days and nights for him. Why did he not push on and capture those murderers? Instead of so doing, the whole command stopped, and spent days and weeks trying men who had willingly given themselves up, leaving their chiefs and bands. I, as a woman, know very little about war; but I know Little Crow and his soldiers might have been captured last fall, but now it is very doubtful if he is ever overtaken. But I suppose the troops were fatigued, if they marched all the way from St. Paul as fast as they did from Yellow Medicine—taking over fifty hours to travel twenty-five miles.

I don't wish to censure those that were compelled to do as they were bidden, but their leaders. If those officers had known their wives and daughters were in danger, they would have found ways and means to travel more than five miles a day.

From the way the affair was conducted, I suppose if Sibley had not found us on that prairie, he would have returned, and we would have passed the winter on the plains; for he went no farther, as he said he could not pursue them without cavalry. He did, after a few weeks had passed, send out scouting parties, when he knew the Indians were returning to surrender. But he nor his troops never captured an Indian, (and I don't believe ever will, until there is change made in our officers,) only those that wished to be taken, they preferring captivity to death by starvation. I never can give Sibley any credit in releasing the prisoners, or capturing Indians, for do you, my readers, consider it a capture when men willingly wait two days and nights for their captors to march twenty-five miles? It was a wonderful affair! Glory, honor, and renown, ought to be written on their brows! God influenced those Indians to remain with us, and to God and the Indians I give my thanks.

After I heard Chaska was in prison, I was unhappy. I felt as if the Indians, as well as myself, had been deceived. All the solemn promises I had made to Chaska were as naught. What would he think of me? I could not eat or sleep, I was so excited about him. I felt as bad as if my brother had been in the same position.

The women knowing I felt sad, tried every way to aggravate me, some saying, "I know he is a murderer. I know he killed my brother, sister, or some other relative." I would reply, "If he has done such things, how could you be so friendly with him?" for these same women would come in and laugh, sing, and play cards with him very often, and Mrs. A——, from the neighborhood of Forest City, used to comb his hair, arrange his neck-tie, and, after he was arrested, abused him shamefully.

When Chaska was to be tried, I was called upon to testify. I told them all I could say would be in his favor. They thought it very strange I could speak in favor of an Indian. I went into court, and was put under oath. Chaska was present, and I shook hands with him. I am particular in relating every interview I had with him, as many false and slanderous stories are in circulation about me.

He was convicted of being an accomplice in the murder of Geo. Gleason, without any evidence against him. I was angry, for it seemed to me as if they considered my testimony of no account; for if they had believed what I said, he would have been acquitted. All the evidence was his own statement, wherein he said that he snapped his gun at Mr. Gleason; but through misrepresentation, it was made to appear as if he intended to try to kill him.

I know he had no more idea of killing the man than I had, or did no more towards it than I did. He was present, so was I; and they might as well hang me as him, for he was as innocent as myself.

After Mr. Gleason was dead, as we road away from his body, I heard Chaska say to Hapa, "Get out and shoot him again; don't leave him with any life to suffer." Hapa said, "You have not shot to-day; you go with me, and I will go." Then they both got out giving me the lines to hold, and went to the body, but it was still and motionless. Hapa fired at him; Chaska raised his gun, but it snapped fire. I don't believe his gun was loaded at all. That was what convicted him. Afterwards, in speaking to me of the affair, he said he had done as he would wish any one to do by him. He was afraid there was a little life, and he wished him put out of suffering.

I know that after he was convicted I said many things I need not have said, and would not at ordinary times; but every one ought to know that my mind was in a dreadful state, living as I had for six weeks in continual fear and anxiety, and I was not capable of acting rationally. The Indian who saved George Spencer's life was lauded to the skies, and I could not refrain from saying that I considered my life and that of my two children as valuable as his; but the Indian that saved me must be imprisoned, while that Indian was carried around and shown as a great hero, and at the same time was known to be the murderer of Mr. Divoll, and at the time George Spencer was wounded, was murdering the whites.[84]

But I soon discovered that the Commission was not acting according to justice, but by favor; and I was terribly enraged against them. The more angry I got, the more I talked, making matters worse for Chaska as well as myself. I can now see wherein I failed to accomplish my object. They soon at the camp began to say that I was in love; that I was his wife; that I preferred living with him to my husband, and all such horrid, abominable reports. I know I am innocent; that I acted from right motives; and sure am I if I am condemned here on earth, God will see me righted—if not here, I hope in Heaven.

I never could love a savage, although I could respect any or all that might befriend me, and I would willingly do everything in my power to benefit those that were so kind to me in my hour of need. I have strong feelings of gratitude towards many of them. I can not feel as many persons do, for I lost no friends, and I was kindly treated by all but Hapa. I feel very sorry for those that have suffered at their hands in any manner. I do not know of but two females that were abused by the Indians. I often asked the prisoners when we met, for we were hearing all kinds of reports, but they all said they were well treated, that I saw. It is true that there were many persons there that I never saw until I was brought into Sibley's camp, for the Indian camp was so large it was like a city, and a person was in danger of losing themselves unless there was something particular that would indicate the locality of the tepee. Many kept small white flags and such things flying, to notify members of the family where their homes were.

I think it was two days before I left Camp Release that I went to the Indian camp. Miss E. B—— accompanied me. I saw Chaska's mother, and such a cry as burst from her at the sight of me. She put her arms around me, saying, "My boy! my boy! they will kill him! Why don't you save him? He saved your life many times. You have forgotten the Indians now your white friends have come." I was much affected at her reproaches, and I told her I was doing everything I could to save him, but the Indians were lying about him. She told me she had been to carry him some bread, but the soldiers would not let her go in where he was, and she begged me to go and see him. I had not been to see the prisoners until that day, although the women were going several times every day. I had always refused, for I knew it would make me feel sad to see those who had been so kind to me tied together like beasts, and felt that they would reproach me for not trying to assist them, now they were in danger.

This day, when I returned to camp, I went to the prisoners tent, accompanied by Major Cullen and Miss E. B——.[85] When I entered I went towards Chaska to shake hands, but he refused to take my hand. I inquired what was the cause of this acting so unfriendly. He said I had told falsehoods to the soldiers, or I would not now see him tied hand and foot. He then repeated all he had done for me and my children, and reproached me for so soon forgetting his kindness. It affected me to tears, for he spoke of many things he had done, such as selling his coat for flour, sleeping without his blanket so my children might be warm, &c. I said to him that I had lost all my friends now by trying to save him, and it was very wrong for him to blame me. I am not ashamed to acknowledge that I cried. I am naturally very sensitive, and cannot see tears or hear reproaches without shedding tears.

I at last convinced him that I was not to blame for his imprisonment, and I said I would like to shake hands and bid him goodbye in friendship. He shook hands with me, and that is all that passed between us. I never saw him again, for I left very soon for my home.

There were at that time twenty-one Indians all fastened together by their feet. I did not go any nearer to him than four feet, but there have been outrageous reports put in circulation of that visit I made that poor forsaken creature. Any one doubting my story may inquire of the persons who were with me—not of the soldiers. I was not aware of the excitement that existed throughout the country. I knew there had been awful murders committed, but I knew not the particulars, or how people were enraged against the Indians. I was so happy, and rejoiced so greatly, over my safe deliverance from death and dishonor, through the kindness of the Indians, that I wished to sound their praises far and near.

That night before leaving, I heard from Capt. Grant that Chaska would not be executed, but would be imprisoned for five years. I was very well contented, and troubled myself no farther, for he gave me his word as a gentleman that that was the truth. He cautioned me not to speak of it, as it was a secret. I never told any one until he was dead.

I came from Camp Release with four ladies who had been prisoners. We were sent without any escort over seventy miles, through the scene of those awful murders. The day before we left, Sibley sent down a train of forty wagons, and a number of prisoners, mostly French and Germans, with eighty soldiers as an escort. When we got to Yellow Medicine I found them there, on their way to Wood Lake to camp for the night, and we ladies proposed camping with them, as the man who drove our team said he was going to Redwood to camp, saying there was no danger, for there were no Indians within one hundred miles of us, except those at Camp Release.[86] I got frightened, as usual, and said I was afraid to go on to Redwood to camp; for I had suffered so much in that neighborhood I cared not to stay there over night; so I concluded to leave the horse team, and stay with the ox train, as I saw a lady in the train that I knew very well. Mrs. H—— and I remained at the soldiers' camp until after supper, when we proposed to go back to Yellow Medicine—three miles distant—and stay in the tepees, for my baby was very low, and I did not dare to stay out all night without some covering, for our blankets we had left at Camp Release, as they were borrowed from the soldiers, and the tents the soldiers had up were just large enough for four persons sitting, no fire in them, and the wind was blowing a hurricane, for it was now October. My children were both without shirts, Nellie had a dress, no shoes or stockings, nor anything

Plenty (1862), a Dakota captured by Gen. H. H. Sibley's forces but not hanged. Photo not attributed, Minnesota Historical Society.

else. My boy had an Indian jacket and leggings. I knew we would be comfortable at the tepees, and there were several half-breeds there who could speak English as well as myself.

The farmer Indians were at Yellow Medicine under Major Galbraith's directions, digging potatoes. We went to John Moore's tepee, and stayed with his family all night. Capt. McClarthy promised to wait for us; but when we arrived at the camp they had all gone.[87] Not a vestige of the camp was discernible.

I afterwards learned that the wagon master, hearing of our going to the tepees, said he would hurry on; and if we liked the tepees so well, we might stay there, for he was going to hurry off.

Capt. Kennedy and one of his soldiers were detailed to come for us in the morning from the camp of soldiers that were guarding the Indians, and they were only ordered to take us to Wood Lake.[88] Now we were in great trouble; they dared not go any farther without orders, and we did not wish to stay at the tepees. The soldiers at length decided to go on with us to Fort Ridgely without orders, thinking we could overtake the other teams when they stopped for dinner at Redwood. Mrs. H—— and myself traveled in great fear all day. I was now going toward the spot where poor Gleason was killed, and she where her husband laid, still unburied. We imagined Indians in every bush. We had but one gun, and now I think how reckless we were to start on such a journey in such an unprotected way.

The men laughed at our fears, but I told them Mr. Gleason also laughed, going over the same road; and I felt sure there were Indians now near us, for Little Crow sent out one hundred men the night before the battle of Wood Lake, and they had never returned to camp. No one can imagine my feelings as I passed poor Gleason's grave, for he was now covered from sight; the whole scene was again before my eyes. I got so nervous that my teeth chattered, and I shook like one with the palsy. As we got to the river, my fears increased, for it was a dreary place. Now we had to go down through the woods for some ways, and we all expected to be fired upon by Indians hiding in the bushes; but God in his mercy delivered us from death by them, for it afterwards proved that Indians were secreted in those woods. We at last arrived at Little Crow's village; the buildings were all standing, and everything was looking well, only so desolate; not a sound to break the stillness, not a living thing visible. The soldiers proposed leaving the road and going to a farm house to get some corn for their horses, for we had all come without breakfast. We sat in the wagon, Mrs. H., myself and children, while they gave their horses feed; and while they were eating, the men roamed through the gardens, gathering tomatoes, &c. In a few minutes after they left we heard a dog bark, and I told Mrs. H. there were Indians in the neighborhood. In a moment we heard a gun, and then another; Mrs. H—— being much alarmed, jumped and ran into a corn field. As she did so I saw two Indians just going down into the woods not ten rods from where we sat. I beckoned to the men, and they very hurriedly hitched up the horses, and they drove them on a run for the other teams which we had seen some three miles beyond us, on a hill.

The soldiers' object in going that way was to save five miles, but we came near losing our lives by so doing. As we drove over the prairie, regardless of road or track, we turned, and five Indians were coming toward us on foot running very fast. About that time, the teams on the hill seeing us, and thinking we were Indians, started some men to capture us. The Indians, seeing the horsemen, turned around and made for the woods, where we could see their tepees. We were very glad to meet with the train, and we arrived at the Fort at 5 o'clock that evening, very tired, but O, how happy to be within its walls. How refreshing that bath, and the clean clothes, given us by the kind lady of the Surgeon, and with what feelings of joy I laid myself and little ones down to rest, undressed—it being the first time I had taken my clothes off to sleep, in nearly eight weeks. The next morning, as Mrs. H—— and I were preparing for breakfast, my little boy exclaimed, "There is my father!"—and so it was. There was my husband I had mourned as dead, now living—coming toward me. I was happy then, and felt that I would have died then willingly, and said, "Thy will not mine be done," for I knew my children had a protector now.

I left the Fort about noon that day, and arrived at Shakopee in a few days. I did not hear any more respecting Chaska, but felt it was all right with him. I was in Red Wing when the President sent on the list of those who were to be executed. I noticed the name of Chaskadon, but knew it was not Chaska's number, and that he was not guilty of the crime that Chaskadon was to be punished for.[89]

Sunday after the execution, when the papers were brought in, I noticed my name immediately, and I then saw that a mistake had been made. The Indian name Chaskadon, that the President ordered to be hanged, killed a pregnant woman and cut out her child, and they hung Chaska who was only convicted of being present when Mr. Gleason was killed.

After passing eight weeks in Red Wing, I returned to St. Paul. I then saw Rev. S. R. Riggs, formerly missionary among the Sioux, and who was present at the time Chaska was hung, and he said he was really hanged by mistake, as his name was on the list that were recommended to mercy. In a letter I received from him, he explained the matter in this way:

"MRS. WAKEFIELD—*Dear Madam:*—In regard to the mistake by which Chaska was hung instead of another, I doubt whether I can satisfactorily explain it. We all felt a solemn responsibility, and a fear that some mistake should occur. We had forgotten that he was condemned under the name of We-chan-hpe-wash-tay-do-pe.[90] We knew

Soldiers guarding Dakota captives at the Lower Agency, late fall, 1862. The photo was taken in front of the log trading post of François La Bathe. Photo, Whitney's Gallery, Minnesota Historical Society.

he was called Chaska in the prison, and had forgotten that any other except Robert Hopkins, who lived by Dr. Williamson, was so called.[91] We never thought of the third one; so when the name Chaska was called in the prison on that fatal morning, your protector answered to it and walked out. I do not think any one was really to blame. We all regretted the mistake very much, &c.

"With kind respects, yours truly,
"S. R. RIGGS."

Now I will never believe that all in authority at Mankato had forgotten what Chaska was condemned for, and I am sure, in my own mind, it was done intentionally. I dare not say by whom, but there is One who knoweth every secret, either good or bad, and the time will come when he will meet that murdered man, and then he will find the poor Indian's place is far better than his own.

If the President had not plainly stated what the man was convicted for, then, probably, there might have been a mistake made, but as it was, it was either carelessness, or, as I said before, intentional: for every man was numbered as he was arrested, and the President sent

Chaska, ca. 1860. Photo, C. A. Zimmerman, Minnesota Historical Society [E91.1C/r8]. Because the name Chaska means "first-born son" and because there are potentially thousands of men with this name and many more with variations of this name, it is impossible to say with accuracy that the photograph used here is the Dakota man Chaska who was Wakefield's "protector," but it appears plausible that this is the Chaska in question.

the number, as well as the cause of his punishment. It has caused me to feel very unkindly towards my own people, particularly those in command at Mankato. There have been all kinds of reports in circulation respecting Chaska and myself, but I care not for them. I know that I did what was right, that my feelings were only those of gratitude toward my preserver. I should have done the same for the blackest negro that Africa ever produced; I loved not the man, but his kindly acts.

I know that many Indians now paid by Government are murderers, but being connected with the officers by blood are saved, while the true-hearted full blood savage has been hung for these men's crimes. I know of one who came into a tepee one night. He had not seen me in a squaw dress, and did not know but what I was a squaw. He then and there related scenes that made my very blood curdle in my veins. He told of meeting a mother and three children, and after violating the oldest daughter, who was about fourteen years old, he beat them all to death with a club. When the Indians asked why he did it, he said they were only Dutch, and it was just like killing hogs. He now calls himself a friendly Indian, or a white man, as he is three-fourths white. Most of the half-breeds are treacherous like him. I would sooner trust a full blood than any of them. When they heard that Sibley's forces were coming, they began to show great feeling for the *poor captives* . Previous to that if a prisoner went to them for protection they were driven away, fearing they might be blamed by the Indians. A Mrs. Earle, who lived near Beaver Creek, with a little girl nine years of age, was held by Little Crow himself.[92] She always stayed in his tepee with his wives. At the time of the battle of Wood Lake, he turned them away, telling them they might find friends elsewhere. They went to John Renville's a half-breed, of whom I have spoken in this work. He said he could not protect them; that they must leave immediately. Mrs. Earle was in great fear. She told them she would not eat much. He said, "No matter! go somewheres! go hide yourself on the prairie!" She started to go, she knew not whither, when she met an Indian who told her to come with him. He took her in, gave her food, and cared for her like a brother, when this part-white man would not do anything for her. Such is the way with the part breeds, or many of them. I would not trust myself with one of them. There is too much art and duplicity in them. All of them helped rob the whites. Now at this time they are bringing large bills against Government for what they have lost, when they have at the same time hundreds of dollars worth of goods stolen from the whites.

There are many things I would like to speak about in this narrative, but I would be obliged to mention particular names, and I will forbear; but I will say this, that many persons told entirely different stories respecting their treatment, after Sibley came, than they did before. One lady very often visited me, and she often complained of being uncomfortable from eating so heartily, but said the squaws forced her to eat, as that is their way of showing their kindness towards a person. Now many times I have listened to her telling the soldiers that she was nearly starved by the squaws, going days without food of any kind. It shocked me, and I reprimanded her severely for telling such untruths; but she was only one of a class of females that were endeavoring to excite the sympathies of the soldiers. My object was to excite sympathy for the Indians and in so doing, the soldiers lost all respect for me, and abused me shamefully; but I had rather have my own conscience than that of those persons who turned against their protectors, those that were so kind to them in that great time of peril.

All the time I was with the Indians the women seemed to be envious of me, saying that the Indians thought more of me than any other female. They did of course think more of me than they did of strangers, for they had known me many years. I could talk with them of things that had transpired in Shakopee that they knew about, and they considered me an old friend. No Indian ever came to my house hungry without being fed, or if in need of clothes, I gave if I possibly could do so. They all came to me for medicine as much as they did to my husband, both in Shakopee and Yellow Medicine, and their actions have proved the bible true to me, for it says, "Cast your bread upon the water, and after many days it shall return to you."

I will draw my work to conclusion by giving an account of my husband's escape from Yellow Medicine on Tuesday, August 19th, He says that soon after I left, Mr. Garvie came to the Agency, informing them that the Indians were returning from above, and he was afraid they intended mischief. Soon after he left, Akepa and Other Day came in, and said the Indians were going to make an attack that night. The inhabitants were all soon assembled together in the ware house, every one ready to protect him or herself, the friendly Indians remaining with them. Soon after dark they heard reports of guns, and they knew they had attacked the trading post, under the hill. One by one the friendly Indians left, except Other Day. Having a white wife, I presume, kept him from going. They were in great fear, expecting every moment to be attacked. Very often during the night some three or four Indians would ascend the hill, look towards the buildings, then retire, seeming to be keeping an eye on them. What must those poor creatures have suffered during that long night! Soon they heard some one at the door, and poor Garvie, wounded and covered with dirt, was found and taken in. He was attended to as well as could be under the circumstances. About daylight some one of the party proposed trying to escape. Other Day was very anxious, and said he could get them across the Minnesota River at an old Indian crossing, but to get there they must ascend a high hill, showing themselves to the Indians in the valley of the Yellow Medicine. But they knew it was death to remain, and they had little, if any, hopes of getting away. The hope was so faint that they did not even take their watches or papers with them. They only had seven vehicles, some only large enough to hold two persons, but they started. The Indians were so busy plundering the stores that they did not notice them. They crossed the river,—sixty-one persons, piloted by Other Day,—and when across they were obliged to stop and cut their road through the thick woods that skirts the north bank of that river. Every stroke of the axe, they thought, would lead to their discovery; but no! They went on; on, on in a very slow way, as they had no roads, as I said before. They did not stop until near midnight, when they camped at a deserted house. The women made a few biscuits out of flour and water,

but they did not want much, for a person has no appetite when they are
fleeing for their lives. They remained there the remainder of the night,
and in the morning they again started, not having seen or heard any
Indians, Other Day going two or three miles in advance of the train,
trying to beat up the enemy if any were hidden. They rode all day in
great excitement, and at night arrived at a place called Cedar City.
Here they found quite a party of setters trying to fortify the place.
They remained together all night. In the morning when they were
about to leave, Mr. Garvie requested to be left, saying he would die if
he rode farther, jolting over the rough roads. Bidding him be careful,
they again started, going right through the Big Woods, past the scene
of many murders; but still an All-wise Providence kept them from all
harm. They arrived at Chaska on Saturday morning, after traveling
four days and nights, expecting every moment to be struck down by
some foe. My husband came into Shakopee, holding in his hands an account of his own death, as it was reported they were all killed. He had
on at the time of the outbreak, a thin suit of clothes and a pair of slip-
pers, as the day had been extremely warm, and when he got down to
Shakopee he was barefoot; everything gone: wife, children, home,
property,—all he then thought destroyed by the Indians. But through
God's mercy we were all saved, and are now re-united.

In conclusion, I will say that the Indian Expedition of this year
has not accomplished any thing of importance.[93] They met the Indians, had a few skirmishes, driving them across the Missouri River. Dr.
Weiser, of Shakopee, was killed, being shot down by some Indians with
whom he was conversing in a friendly manner.[94] This brought on a
fight. If this *had not occurred* there would not have been any fight; for
Sibley would have had a parley and the Indians would have been
brought down and been fed and *petted* as those were last winter. They
did take Little Crow's son, who from starvation and fatigue had secreted himself in the grass. This is all that has been done by this large
force. Another year the scenes of the two last years will be repeated,
and this war will be prolonged for many, many years, unless we have a
change of officers. The army on the Missouri, under Gen. Sully, has
done a good work, killing many Indians and destroying their property,
while our army has been only enriching the officers, and shielding
murderers from justice.[95] An account I have received from the new
agency is not very good. The land is very poor. The Indians cannot
raise any thing only on the bottom lands. The water is all alkali, causing the deaths of many after they reached there. The Indians are all
dissatisfied, and the Winnebagoes are building canoes and threaten to

leave very soon.[96] They have no good hunting grounds unless they cross the Missouri River, and there they are in danger of being killed by the Brules and Tetons, who are at war with them.[97] So this poor down-trodden race is in a dreadful condition. They must starve unless food is sent them by Government. There is at the Agency 3,600 Indians. Three missionaries are with them, and more are still going. But what a place for white people where nothing can be raised! I think they have begun to realize some of the sufferings I often tried to point out to them during my stay with them.

Their reservation in this State was a portion of the most beautiful country that was ever known, and they had everything they wished to make them comfortable if they could have only stayed there; but a few evil men commenced their murderous work, and all has gone to ruin. I feel very sorry for many of my neighbors who for years have lived like the white man; now they are wanderers, without home, or even a resting place. A few days since a number of families passed through here, and as I saw them I ran with eagerness to see those old faces who were so kind to me while I was in captivity. I went down to the camp (for they stayed all night in Shakopee), and was rejoiced to be able to take them some food, and other little things which I knew would please them, and for this I have been blamed; but I could not help it. They were kind to me, and I will try and repay them, trusting that in God's own time I will be righted and my conduct understood, for with Him all things are plain. And now I will bid this subject farewell forever

THE END

NOTES

1. I dislike the term "mixed-blood," but writing out "mixed racial and ethnic" or "intermarried" or other terms is awkward, and "mixed-blood" is the common term. We need a new term. One of the thirty-nine condemned men, "Godfrey, a Negro," was given a last-minute reprieve. For an overview, see June Namias, *White Captives: Gender and Ethnicity on the American Frontier* (Chapel Hill: University of North Carolina Press, 1993), 219–28; and Gary Clayton Anderson, *Kinsmen of Another Kind: Dakota-White Relations in the Upper Mississippi Valley, 1650–1862* (Lincoln: University of Nebraska Press, 1984).

2. *New York Times*, August 24, August 25, August 29, 1862; *Harper's Weekly*, September 13, 1862, 592.

3. H. H. Sibley to Sarah Sibley, from Camp Lincoln, November 12, 1862, Henry Hasting Sibley Papers, 1815–1930, Minnesota Historical Society (hereafter Sibley Papers, MHS), microfilm. According to W. W. Folwell, the people of New Ulm were reburying their dead on the days the group came through the town. William Watts Folwell, *A History of Minnesota* [1924], rev. ed., vol. 2 (St. Paul: Minnesota Historical Society Press, 1978), 200–201.

4. S. R. Riggs to S. B. Treat, November 24, 1862, Stephen R. Riggs Papers; and Thomas Williamson to S. B. Treat, December 1, 1862, Thomas S. Williamson Papers, both in the collections of the American Board of Commissioners for Foreign Missions (hereafter ABCFM), Houghton Library, Harvard University.

5. The letter and the list of accused, along with those charged, were all published, December 11, 1862, in Records of the Trial of Sioux-Dakota Indians in Minnesota, 1862, 37th Congress, 3d Session (hereafter "Records of the Trial"), Ex. Doc. 1, and D, and 6–7. There is some reason to suspect that more than two women were sexually abused. Mrs. N. D. [Urania S. Frazer] White, "Captivity among the Sioux, August 18 to September 26, 1862," *Minnesota Historical So-*

ciety Collections 9 (April 1901): 395–426. The rape cases include Case Nos. 12, 4, and 22, SEN 37A-F2 44D, in National Archives (hereafter NA) Record Group 46, 37th Congress, "Presidential Messages transmitted to the Senate, 1789–1875," Records of the Military Commission that tried Sioux-Dakota Indians for barbarities committed in Minnesota, 1862 (unpublished manuscript).

6. The M. S. Wilkinson, Cyrus Aldrich, and William Windom letter to President Lincoln is in "Message of the President of the United States in Answer to the Resolution of the Senate of the 5th Instant in Relation to the Indian Barbarities in Minnesota," December 11, 1862, in Records of the Trial, Ex. Doc. 7, C, 2–3. The letter was also run in several major Minnesota newspapers.

7. Ibid., 3.

8. Ibid.

9. Ibid., 4.

10. Isaac V. D. Heard, *History of the Sioux War and Massacres of 1862 and 1863* (1864; reprint, Milwood, N.Y.: Krause Reprint, 1975), 287; *Harper's Weekly*, December 20, 1862. Rape is discussed by Stephen R. Riggs in *Mary and I: Forty Years with the Sioux* (Chicago: W. G. Holmes, 1889), 180. On rape cases, see NA Record Group 46, Case No. 2 against Te-he-hdo-ne-cha; Case No. 4 against Ta-zoo, or Ptandoota; and Case No. 22 against Do-Wan-Sa. All three men were hanged at Mankato. The rape issue is highly contested. George Spencer, a white clerk who was captured and was one of the few white men in the camp of Little Crow and the Dakotas in rebellion, claimed that though he was treated well, "the female captives were, with very few exceptions, subjected to the the most horrible treatment. In some cases a woman would be taken into the woods and her person violated by 6, 7, and as many as 10 or 12 of these fiends at one time." NA Record Group 48, entry no. 663, Sioux Commission, 1863, and George H. Spencer, Jr., 1862, 15, in *The Court Proceedings in the Trial of Dakota Indians Following the Massacre in Minnesota in August 1862* (Minneapolis: Satterlee Printing, 1927), 9–11, in Minnesota Historical Society (hereafter MHS). In a letter to his wife, Col. H. H. Sibley wrote, "There is one young lady, very respectable and of fine personal appearance, a Miss Williams, who has been very much abused; indeed I think all the young ones have been." The reference is to Matty Williams. See Sibley Papers, MHS, September 27, 1862.

11. Roy W. Meyer, *History of the Santee Sioux: United States Indian Policy on Trial* (Lincoln: University of Nebraska Press, 1967), 146–54, and Meyer letter to the editor, October, 23, 1995.

12. Adam Kuper, *The Invention of Primitive Society: Transformations of an Illusion* (New York: Routledge, 1988), 1–14, 42–75, esp. 66, 231–44, esp. 240; and Roy Harvey Pearce, *The Savages of America: A Study of the Indian and the Idea of Civilization*, rev. ed. (Baltimore: Johns Hopkins Press, 1988).

13. Raymond DeMallie, comments to the editor, fall, 1995; Meyer, *History of Santee Sioux*, 5. Herbert T. Hoover finds that only the Mdewakantons and Wahpekutes can be called Santees. Letter and comments to the editor, November 20, 1995. See Ruth Underhill, *Red Man's America: A History of Indians in the United States*, rev. ed. (Chicago: University of Chicago Press, 1971); and

John R. Swanton, "Dakota," *The Indian Tribes of North America* (Washington, D.C.: U.S. Government Printing Office, 1952), 280–85, and in the same work, "Mdewakanton," 827–29. On contemporary name changes and affiliation, see Patricia C. Albers and William R. James, "On the Dialectics of Ethnicity: To Be or Not to Be Santee (Sioux)," *Journal of Ethnic Studies* 14 (Spring 1986): 1–28, esp. 1–7, 14–15. See entry on Sioux, in *Encyclopedia of American Indian History,* ed. Frederick E. Hoxie (Boston: Houghton Mifflin, 1996).

14. Herbert T. Hoover, *The Yankton Sioux* (New York: Chelsea House, 1988), 13–14; and Samuel Pond, *The Dakota or Sioux in Minnesota as They Were in 1834* [1908], introduction Gary Clayton Anderson (St. Paul: Minnesota Historical Society Press, 1986); and Gary Clayton Anderson, *Little Crow: Spokesman for the Sioux* (St. Paul: Minnesota Historical Society Press, 1986), 1. Hoover, letter to the editor, cites the thirty thousand figure from Stephen Riggs.

15. Helen Hornbeck Tanner, *The Ojibwa,* (New York: Chelsea House, 1992), 43–44; David Wooley, "The Santee Sioux: The Newcomers," *The First Voices, NABRASKAland Magazine* 62 (January-February 1984), 38–39; and Rev. Edward D. Neill, *The History of Minnesota from the French Explorations to the Present Time,* 5th ed. (Minneapolis: Minnesota Historical Society Press, 1883), 128–33.

16. Meyer, *History of Santee Sioux,* 18; Anderson, *Kinsmen,* 59–60, 65, 76; Anderson, *Little Crow,* 9; David I. Bushnell Jr., "Seth Eastman: The Master Painter of the North American Indian," *Smithsonian Miscellaneous Collections* 87, no. 3 (April 11, 1932). 2–3. For more on French influence and the interconnections between the trading system and social systems along the Mississippi, especially in the South, see Daniel H. Usner Jr., *Indians, Settlers, and Slaves in a Frontier Exchange Economy: The Lower Mississippi Valley before 1783* (Chapel Hill: University of North Carolina Press, 1992).

17. Francis Paul Prucha, *The Great Father: The United States Government and the American Indians,* abbrev. ed. (Lincoln: University of Nebraska Press, 1986), 18; Kenneth M. Morrison, "Native Americans and the American Revolution. Historic Stories and Shifting Frontier Conflict," in *Indians in American History: An Introduction,* ed. Frederick E. Hoxie (Arlington Heights, Ill.: Harlan Davidson, 1988), 112–13; Colin G. Calloway, *The American Revolution in Indian Country: Crisis and Diversity in Native American Communities* (New York: Cambridge University Press, 1995), 281, 190–91.

18. See R. David Edmunds, *Tecumseh and the Quest for Indian Leadership* (New York: Harper Collins, 1984); and Gregory Evans Dowd, *A Spirited Resistance: The North American Indian Struggle for Unity, 1745–1815* (Baltimore: Johns Hopkins Press, 1992).

19. Anthony F. C. Wallace, *The Long, Bitter Trail: Andrew Jackson and the Indians* (New York: Hill and Wang, 1993), 26–35; Prucha, *Great Father,* abbrev. ed., 91–99.

20. By the 1850s the Upper Agency Dakotas were predominantly members of the Sisseton and Wahpeton bands. Samuel Pond found the different bands of Dakotas to be so intermingled that it was "impossible to ascertain

their exact numbers." Pond, *Dakota*, 5. Alan Woolworth mentioned the figure nineteen hundred (in 1861) in a telephone conversation with the editor, July 26, 1991, but Ruth Landes finds Santee bands in the Mdewakanton villages ranging from under fifty to four hundred in *The Mystic Lake Sioux: Sociology of the Mdewakanton Santee* (Madison: University of Wisconsin Press, 1968), 13–14. See also Richard White, *The Middle Ground: Indians, Empires, and Republics in the Great Lakes Region, 1650–1815* (New York: Cambridge University Press, 1991), 486, 518–23.

21. Prucha, *Great Father*, abbrev. ed., map of factory system, 1795–1822, 37, 57–59. Although the hope that Indians would become like whites existed from colonial days and the Jeffersonian era, the "civilization program" began in earnest after 1819. Francis Paul Prucha, "United States Indian Policies, 1815–1860," in Handbook of North American Indians, vol. 4, *History of Indian-White Relations*, ed. Wilcomb E. Washburn (Washington, D.C.: Smithsonian Institution, 1988), 43. The contemporary name of the Office of Indian Affairs is the Bureau of Indian Affairs (BIA).

22. Anderson, *Kinsmen*, 74–75.

23. Ibid., 82–83, 92–94; Wallace, *Long, Bitter Trail*, 30–35. Prucha calls the 1820s a period of crisis in "United States Indian Policies," 43–47.

24. Prairie du Chien divided the two groups, designating as Ojibwa hunting grounds much of the northern part of Minnesota and giving the Dakotas most of the lands in the southern half of the state. Anderson, *Kinsmen*, 122–23. Tanner describes the festive gathering that accompanied the treaty of 1825 in *Ojibwa*, 72–74, using James O. Lewis's drawing of the event. According to Herbert T. Hoover, an 1839 census counted 1,658 Mdewakantons and a total of 3,989 Dakota Indians "in the fur trade area between Fort Snelling and the James River Basin." See Hoover, "Dakota," *Native America in the Twentieth Century, An Encyclopedia* (New York: Garland Publishing, 1994), 161.

25. Anderson, *Kinsmen*, 153–55.

26. Ibid., 177; raw total from Series A 195–209, "Population of States, by Sex, Race, Urban-Rural Residence, and Age: 1790–1970," in Ben J. Wattenberg, *The Statistical History of the United States: From Colonial Times to the Present,* (New York: Basic Bods, 1976), 30, 37. See chart, Minnesota Population, 1850–1870, in June Namias, "White Captives: Gender and Ethnicity on Successive American Frontiers, 1607–1862," Ph.D. diss., Brandeis University, 1988, 584–87. Prucha sees the failure of the removal policy as related to the continual white move west, which he feels fostered "new circumstances" in which whites demanded the "concentration" of Indians. Prucha, "U.S. Indian Policies," 47–48. The present city of Shakopee was named for a chief by the name of Shakopee, or Shakpay; it is located south and west of St. Paul. Shakopee's village was located on the Minnesota River by the Redwood River, north and west of New Ulm and Fort Ridgely. In earlier times Shakopee's village on the Minnesota River was a summer camp for his band and the village in south central Minnesota, near present-day St. Paul, was the winter camp, although by the mid-nineteenth century, the people used both year round.

27. Anderson, *Kinsmen*, 179.

28. Prucha, "U.S. Indian Policies," 50.

29. Anderson, *Kinsmen*, 217–18.

30. Francis Paul Prucha, *The Great Father: The United States Government and the American Indians*, 2 vols. (Lincoln: University of Nebraska Press, 1995), 439. Citations from June 19, 1858, treaty with the Mdewakanton and Wahpekutes from Charles J. Kappler, comp., *Indian Affairs: Laws and Treaties*, vol. 2 (Washington, D.C.: Government Printing Office, 1904), 781–89. Galbraith quote from "Commissioner of Indian Affairs: Report for the 1863, January 27, 1863" in Prucha, *Great Father*, 439.

31. Minnesota entered the Union on May 11, 1858. For information on this phase of Indian affairs, see Prucha, *Great Father*, abbrev. ed., 100–11; Anderson, *Kinsmen*, chap. 11, esp. 246; and David A. Nichols, *Lincoln and the Indians: Civil War Policy and Politics* (Columbia: University of Missouri Press, 1978), 5–24. The change in agents is mentioned by Big Eagle (Wamditanka), a Mdewakanton chief, in "Chief Big Eagle's Story of the Sioux Outbreak of 1862," *Minnesota Historical Society Collections* 6 (1894): 382–401, esp. 387; and in Gary Clayton Anderson and Alan R. Woolworth, eds., *Through Dakota Eyes: Narrative Accounts of the Minnesota Indian War of 1862* (St. Paul: Minnesota Historical Society Press, 1988), 19–31. For the official discussions by the Indian Affairs establishment, see *Report of the Commissioner of Indian Affairs for the Year 1862* (Washington, D.C.: U.S. Government Printing Office, 1863), 11–23, 49–69.

32. Namias, *White Captives*, 211–13. In the election of 1860, Minnesota gave Lincoln 22,069 votes as against 11,920 for Douglas. Fewer than a thousand combined votes went for John Breckenridge and John Bell.

33. As to the Dakota population, Hoover suggests that Indian Agent Lawrence Taliaferro's 1839 estimate of "slightly fewer than 4,000" Dakotas would still hold in 1860. That estimate makes the 1,658 Mdewakantons the largest of the four groups, with 1,256 Sissetons, 550 Wahpetons, and 325 Wahpekutes (who had suffered from a smallpox epidemic). Hoover, letter to the editor, November 20, 1995. Numbers were gathered by the Indian agent at annuity time. Alan Woolworth, letter to the editor August 17, 1995. Recall that Ruth Landes found the Santee bands among the Mdewakanton villages ranging from under fifty to four hundred. Landes *Mystic Lake Sioux*, 13–14. On the controversy of the role of the Civil War male population drop in Minnesota, see *Minnesota History* (Summer 1976), esp. Priscilla Ann Russo, "The Time to Speak Is Over: The Onset of the Sioux Uprising," *Minnesota History* 45 (Summer 1976): 97–106.

34. There were actually three Shakopees. The first was mentioned by Lt. Zebuleon Pike on his reconnoitering of the upper Mississippi in 1805. The man (also called Six) and his band lived along the Minnesota River. Then there was his son Shakopee (also Shakpay, Shapaydan, or Little Six), who is mentioned by Rev. Samuel Pond as living, in the summer village on the Minnesota River in the 1830s. Pond wrote that he was of the Tintatonwan band and that he was "perhaps the most widely known of the Medawakantonwan [sic] chiefs." This

Shakopee died in 1857. His son, also a chief and also called Shakopee (or Little Six), was called by Pond "a cipher, without character or influence." This Shakopee lived during the uprising and he was executed at Fort Snelling in 1866. See Pond, *Dakota*, 6, 12, 13; and Anderson, *Kinsmen*, 79–80, 236, 266.

35. For the war's onset, see Namias, *White Captives*, 214–19. As to Myrick's statement: Anderson's research indicates that it was probably said sometime between August 5 and 8. Anderson, *Kinsmen*, 250–53.

36. Namias, *White Captives*, 214–19. For Dakota perspectives on the war's causes see "Big Eagle's Story," in Anderson and Woolworth, eds., *Through Dakota Eyes*. Also see Duane P. Schultz, *Over the Earth I Come: The Great Sioux Uprising of 1862* (New York: St. Martin's Press, 1992).

37. Folwell, *History of Minnesota*, vol. 2, 109–10; Kenneth Carley, *The Sioux Uprising of 1862* (St. Paul: Minnesota Historical Society Press, 1976), and Anderson, *Kinsmen*.

38. Pond, *Dakota*, 85–86, 105–10.

39. Eastman was taught the traditional ways but was later educated at Dartmouth and Boston University, where he studied medicine and became a doctor. Married to Elaine Goodale Eastman, he was a man who bridged two cultures. Charles Alexander Eastman (Ohiyesa), *Indian Boyhood* [1902] (Williamstown, Mass.: Corner House Publishers, 1975), 14–21. See Raymond Wilson, *Ohiyesa: Charles Eastman, Santee Sioux* Also see Hertha Dawn Wong, *Sending My Heart Back across the Years: Tradition and Innovation in Native American Autobiography* (New York: Oxford University Press, 1992), 139–52, esp. 151. Charles Alexander Eastman (Ohiyesa), *The Soul of the Indian: An Interpretation* [1911] (Lincoln: University of Nebraska Press, 1980), 3–23.

40. See James R. Walker, "Good Seat, *Wakan Tanka*," in *Lakota Belief and Ritual*, ed. Raymond J. DeMallie and Elaine A. Jahner (Lincoln: University of Nebraska Press, 1980), 70–71. Dr. James R. Walker lived with the Oglala Sioux. Although from a later period and based on a group of Sioux from the plains, some of his work may be relevant. See also Åke Hultkrantz, *The Religions of the American Indians*, trans. Monica Setterwall (Berkeley: University of California Press, 1967), 9–14.

41. George Sword, "Foundations. September 5, 1896," in DeMallie and Jahner, *Lakota Belief*, 74–75; John G. Neihardt, *Black Elk Speaks: Being the Life Story of a Holy Man of the Oglala Sioux* (Lincoln: University of Nebraska Press, 1979), 4–5. See versions of the White Buffalo Woman story in Richard Erdoes and Alfonso Ortiz, eds., *American Indian Myths and Legends* (New York: Pantheon, 1984); Raymond J. DeMallie, "Kinship and Biology in Sioux Culture," in *North American Indian Anthropology: Essays on Society and Culture*, ed. Raymond J. DeMallie and Alfonso Ortiz (Norman: University of Oklahoma Press, 1994), 125–46, esp. 125–30, 142. DeMallie questions whether we can generalize "from Teton data to the Santees" and is uncertain whether the story of White Buffalo Calf Woman was shared, but other Dakotas have told me the story is widely accepted. DeMallie, May 16, 1996, note to the editor. Many of the pipe rituals are still followed by Dakota and Lakota people.

42. Pond, *Dakota*, 93–97. See Calvin Martin, *Keepers of the Game: Indian-Animal Relationships and the Fur Trade* (Berkeley: University of California Press, 1978); and William Cronon, *Changes in the Land: Indians, Colonists, and the Ecology of New England* (New York: Hill and Wang, 1983), 34–53. Russell J. Barber, "Subsistence," in *American Indians: Ready Reference*, vol. 3, ed. Harvey Markowitz (Pasadena, Calif.: Salem Press, 1995), 754–59. On calendric rituals in Seneca society, see Anthony F. C. Wallace, *The Death and Rebirth of the Seneca* (New York: Random-Vintage, 1972).

43. For the particular roles of some of these missionaries in the Dakota trials, see Namias, *White Captives*, 228–37. On the ABCFM, see Michael C. Coleman, *Presbyterian Missionary Attitudes toward American Indians, 1837–1893* (Jackson: University of Mississippi Press, 1985), esp. 3–51. Also see Joan R. Gunderson, "Episcopal Churches on the Minnesota Frontier," *Minnesota History* 50 (Fall 1987), 259–68; and Harvey Markowitz, "The Catholic Mission and the Sioux: A Crisis in the Early Paradigm," in *Sioux Indian Religion*, ed. Raymond J. DeMallie and Douglas R. Parks (Norman: University of Oklahoma Press, 1987, 1987), 113–47. See also Theda Perdue, "Domesticating the Natives: Southern Indians and the Cult of True Womanhood," in *Women, Families, and Communities: Readings in American History Vol. 1: To 1877*, ed. Nancy A. Hewitt (Glenview, Ill.: Scott, Foresman/Little, Brown Higher Education, 1990), 159–70; and Theda Perdue, "Women, Men and American Indian Policy: The Cherokee Response to 'Civilization,'" in *Negotiators of Change: Historical Perspectives on Native American Women*, ed. Nancy Shoemaker (New York: Routledge, 1995), 90–114; Mary E. Young, "Women, Civilization, and the Indian Question," in *Women's America: Refocusing the Past*, ed. Linda K. Kerber and Jane De Hart Mathews (New York: Oxford University Press, 1982), 149–55. On girls' values I have used Marla Powers's work on the Oglala. Although drawn from late-nineteenth-century ethnographies and from a Plains Lakota group, her work rings true for Dakota women. Marla N. Powers, *Oglala Women: Myth, Ritual, and Reality* (Chicago: University of Chicago Press, 1986), 62.

44. DeMallie, "Kinship and Biology," 130, 142. See essays by Arthur Amiotte, Elaine A. Jahner, and Vine V. Deloria, Sr., in DeMallie and Parks, eds., *Sioux Indian Religion*. Also see Åke Hultkrantz, *Native Religions of North America: The Power of Visions and Fertility* (New York: Harper & Row, 1987), and Anderson's interpretation in *Little Crow*. On adoption as a typical part of the captivity practices in the eastern part of the United States, see Namias, *White Captives*, 3–7.

45. See "Big Eagle's Account" (Wamditanka), 23–27, and "Wabasha's Statement," 28–31, both in Anderson and Woolworth, eds., *Through Dakota Eyes*.

46. [Mrs. Mary Rowlandson] *A True History of the Captivity & Restoration of Mrs. Mary Rowlandson* (1682), *Narratives of North American Indian Captivity* (hereafter *Narratives*), reprint vol. 1 (New York: Garland Publishing, 1977); James E. Seaver, *A Narrative of the Life of Mrs. Mary Jemison* [1824], intro. by June Namias, ed. (Norman: University of Oklahoma Press, 1992); Richard Drinnon, ed., *Memoirs of a Captivity among the Indians of North America: John*

Dunn Hunter (1824; reprint, New York: Schocken, 1973); John D. Hunter, *Manners and Customs of Several Indian Tribes Located West of the Mississippi* (1823), *Narratives*, reprint vol. 39 (New York: Garland Publishing, 1977); Richard Slotkin, *Regeneration through Violence: The Mythology of the American Frontier, 1600–1860* (Middletown, Conn.: Wesleyan University Press, 1973). In his work on Mary Rowlandson (forthcoming from Bedford Books), Neal Salisbury notes that even anti-Indian narratives can tell us about Native resistance. "Contextualizing Captivity: Mary Rowlandson among the Nipmucs, Narragansetts, and Wampanoags," paper given for American Society for Ethnohistory, Portland, Oregon, November 8, 1996. I thank Wendy Gamber for giving me a more precise term for these narratives. For an analysis of colonialism and women's autobiography, see Julia Watson and Sidonie Smith, "De/Colonization and the Politics of Discourse in Women's Autobiographical Practices," in *De/Colonizing the Subject: The Politics of Gender in Women's Autobiography*, ed. Sidonie Smith and Julia Watson (Minneapolis: University of Minnesota Press, 1992), xiii–xxxi.

47. Neal Salisbury, review of James Levernier and Hennig Cohen, eds., *The Indians and Their Captives*, in *American Indian Culture and Research Journal* 3, no. 1 (1979): 79–82. Also see Kathryn Zabelle Derounian-Stodala and James Arthur Levernier, *The Indian Captivity Narrative, 1550–1900* (New York: Twayne Publishers, 1993); "Captivity Narratives: Memory, Ethnohistory, or Ethnocentrism?" session at annual meeting of the Organization of American Historians, Chicago, March 26–28, 1996. The John Tanner Project in Winnipeg is verifying the accuracy of the Tanner narrative and using it as a key text in early Canadian history. "Reading John Tanner's Narrative in Context," session at the American Society for Ethnohistory conference, Portland, Oregon, November 9, 1996.

48. *International Genealogical Index.* There is no last name given for Sarah's mother.

49. Although Sarah's family name was Brown, the name "Butts" appears on the territorial and the state marriage certificate. The Scott County Territorial Records, marriage index, 1856; in state listings, April 14, 1865.

50. Scott County, Shakopee, Minnesota, *1860 Census Schedule*, M653 roll 574, enumerated July 27, 1860, 67; Scott County, Shakopee, Minnesota, *1870 Census Schedule*, enumerated Agust 5, 1870.

51. A partial listing of clothing from Sioux Claim of John L. Wakefield (hereafter J. L. Wakefield, Sioux Claim), Sioux Uprising Collection Box 3, J. L. Wakefield, MHS.

52. Ibid.

53. Ibid.

54. Ibid.

55. See the literature on domestic servants, including Hasia Diner, *Erin's Daughters in America: Irish Immigrant Women in the Nineteenth Century* (Baltimore: Johns Hopkins Press, 1983); and Faye E. Dudden, *Serving Women: Household Service in Nineteenth-Century America* (Middletown, Conn.: Wesleyan University Press, 1983), esp. 60–71 on ethnicity and 115–19 on status, also

241–42. For the period 1870–1920, see David M. Katzman, *Seven Days a Week: Women and Domestic Service in Industrializing America* (New York: Oxford University Press, 1978). Also see Phyllis Palmer, *Domesticity and Dirt: Housewives and Domestic Servants in the United States, 1920–1945* (Philadelphia: Temple University Press, 1989), esp. 139–51; and "White Mistress and Black Servant," 184–222.

56. J. L. Wakefield, Sioux Claim. See Wakefield text, as reprinted here, p. 58.

57. Records of the Trial of Sioux-Dakota Indians in Minnesota: Military Commission that tried Sioux-Dakota Indians for barbarities committed in Minnesota, 1862, NA. Record Group 46, 3–5. A telling discussion of "privileged" women and their writings appears in Carolyn Heilbrun's essay in *Life/Lines: Theorizing Women's Autobiography,* ed. Bella Brodzki and Celeste Schenck (Ithaca, N.Y.: Cornell University Press, 1988), 62–76, esp. 65, 76. There Heilbrun presents the notion that such women are "powerless in the midst of their privilege."

58. *Saint Paul Pioneer Press,* May 29, 1899. Wakefield's death was also reported in the St. Paul City Directory. *R. L. Polk & Co's St. Paul City Directory, 1899,* (St. Paul: R. L. Polk, 1899), 1423.

59. Mrs. Sarah F. Wakefield, *Six Weeks in the Sioux Tepees: A Narrative of Indian Captivity* (Shakopee, Minn.: Argus Book and Job Printing Office, 1864), as reprinted here, p. 53.

60. Ibid., as reprinted here, p. 62.

61. On the issue of interracial sex during this period, see Martha Hodes, "Wartime Dialogue on Illicit Sex: White Women and Black Men," in *Divided Houses: Gender and the Civil War,* ed. Catherine Clinton and Nina Silber (New York: Oxford University Press, 1992), 230–42. Hodes calls interracial sex a political issue of the era, noting that the word "miscegenation" is first used in the national political campaign of 1864.

62. Mary Schwandt, "The Story of Mary Schwandt. Her Captivity during the Sioux 'Outbreak,'—1862," *Minnesota Historical Society Collections* 6 (1896): 461–74, esp. 472–73.

63. Wakefield, *Six Weeks* (1864), as reprinted here, pp. 72, 73.

64. Ibid., as reprinted here, pp. 127.

65. Mrs. Sarah F. Wakefield, *Six Weeks in the Sioux Tepees: A Narrative of Indian Captivity* (Minneapolis: Atlas Printing, 1863). The only known copy of the first edition is at the Beinecke Library, Yale University; it is also found in microform in *Western Americana: Frontier History of the Trans-Mississippi West, 1550–1900,* reel 586, no. 6042. Before the networks of mass communication in the East, "book distribution fell largely to itinerant 'hawkers and walkers.'" See Ronald J. Zboray, *A Fictive People: Antebellum Economic Development and the American Reading Public* (New York: Oxford University Press, 1993), "The Book Peddler and Literary Dissemination," 37–54.

66. Wakefield, *Six Weeks,* 1863 and 1864 editions.

67. Wakefield (1864), as reprinted here, p. 77.

68. Ibid., 71.

69. Ibid., 71, 72, 82.

70. Ibid., 79–81.

71. Ibid., 117.

72. See Nina Baym, *Novels, Readers and Reviewers: Responses to Fiction in Antebellum America* (Ithaca, N.V.: Cornell University Press, 1984); and Nina Baym, *Woman's Fiction: A Guide to Novels by and about Women in America, 1820–1870,* 2nd ed. (Urbana: University of Illinois Press, 1993). For the early development of women's writing see Cathy N. Davidson, *Revolution and the Word: The Rise of the Novel in America* (New York: Oxford University Press, 1986). On women's autobiography, see Sidonie Smith, in *The Oxford Companion to Women's Writing in the United States,* ed. Cathy N. Davidson and Linda Wagner-Martin (New York: Oxford University Press, 1995), 85–90; and Sidonie Smith, *A Poetics of Women's Autobiography: Marginality and the Fictions of Self Representation* (Bloomington: University of Indiana Press, 1987).

73. Rose Bluestone, "From My Grandmother I Learned about Sadness," in *Messengers of the Wind: Native American Women Tell Their Life Stories,* ed. Jane Katz (New York: Ballantine Books, 1995), 69–73.

74. I develop these thoughts in "Women as a Moral Force: Indian-White Relations in the Dakota War of 1862," a paper given at Boston College, Chestnut Hill, Massachusetts, at the Society of Historians of the Early Republic (SHEAR) annual meeting, July 16, 1994. I would like to thank Julie Roy Jeffrey, Susan Juster, and those in the audience that day for their comments.

75. Eva Feder Kittay and Diana T. Meyers, eds., *Women and Moral Theory* (Totowa, N.J.: Rowman & Littlefield, 1987), intro., citing Aristotle's *Politics,* Book 13, 14–15.

76. My thoughts here were inspired by William K. Frankena's suggestion that philosophers' arguments be applied to Christian ethics. Here a moral philosopher's approach might be shaped and used to look at historical situations. "Love and Principle in Christian Ethics" in *Perspectives on Morality: Essays by William K. Frankena* (Notre Dame, Ind.: University of Notre Dame Press, 1976), 74–75. Much of Wakefield's narrative reflects in the sentimentality of its day. See Ann Douglas, *The Feminization of American Culture* (New York: Alfred A. Knopf, 1977), 69; Aileen S. Kraditor, ed., *Up from the Pedestal: Selected Writings in the History of American Feminism* (Chicago: Quadrangle Books, 1968), 45–46, 10; Barbara Welter, "The Cult of True Womanhood: 1820–1860," *American Quarterly* 18 (Summer 1966): 151–74; Kathryn Kish Sklar, *Catherine Beecher: A Study in American Domesticity* (New York: W. W. Norton, 1976), 160. For work on morality and women's emergence into the public sphere, see Lori D. Ginzberg, *Women and the Work of Benevolence: Morality, Politics, and Class in the Nineteenth-Century United States* (New Haven. Conn.: Yale University Press, 1990), 9–12, 67, 97–98, 130–32, 213; Mary P. Ryan, *Women in Public: Between Banners and Ballots, 1825–1880* (Baltimore: Johns Hopkins Press, 1990), chaps. 2, 3, 4, esp. 132–35, 142; Linda K. Kerber's analyses of the history of public versus private space in "Separate Spheres, Female Worlds,

Woman's Place: The Rhetoric of Women's History," *Journal of American History* 75 (June 1988): 9–39. On nineteenth-century Western intellectual thought on the subject, see Arthur Schopenhauer, "On Women," in Kittay and Meyers, eds., *Women and Moral Theory,* 14; and Claudia Card, "Gender and Moral Luck," in *Identity, Character, and Morality: Essays in Moral Psychology,* ed. Owen Flanagan and Amélie Oksenberg Rorty (Cambridge, Mass.: MIT Press, 1990), 199–218, esp. 201–2.

77. Carol Gilligan, "In a Different Voice: Women's Conception of Self and Morality," *Harvard Educational Review* 47 (1982): 481–517; and Carol Gilligan, *In a Different Voice: Psychological Theory and Women's Development* (Cambridge, Mass.: Harvard University Press, 1982). According to Kohlberg, the highest level of moral reasoning is based on "universal ethical principles," which are "self-chosen" on the basis of "the universal principles of justice: the equality of human rights and the respect for the dignity of human beings as individual persons." Lawrence Kohlberg, "Moral Stages and Moralization: The Cognitive-Developmental Approach," in *Moral Development and Behavior: Theory, Research, and Social Issues,* ed. Thomas Lickona (New York: Holt, Rinehart and Winston, 1976), 31–53, esp. 31–32, 34–35.

78. Carol Gilligan, "Moral Orientation and Moral Development," in Kittay and Meyers, eds., *Women and Moral Theory,* 19–33; also see Kittay and Meyers's introduction to *Women and Moral Theory,* 3–16, esp. 4–7. Sara Ruddick, "Remarks on the Sexual Politics of Reason," in Kittay and Meyers, eds., *Women and Moral Theory,* 237–60, esp. 237.

79. I would like to thank Peter Iverson (comments at the Western Social Science Association Conference in Denver, April 28, 1988) for pointing out that Mary Butler Renville, a woman captured from S. R. Riggs's Hazelwood mission, five miles above Yellow Medicine, also spoke of white responsibilities toward the Dakotas. Renville kept a diary and claimed her narrative was written from it. Mrs. Mary Butler Renville, *A Thrilling Narrative of Indian Captivity* (Minneapolis: Atlas Company's Books and Job Office, 1863), and Widener microforms, film A 322, reel 443, no. 4491. Widener Library, Harvard University. Wakefield and Renville shared the same publisher, and their narratives both came out the year after the "outbreak." However, Renville never stood as a witness for the Dakotas nor was the main idea of her narrative to defend the remaining Dakotas in Minnesota. On the trial, see NA Record Group 46, SEN 37A-F2, Case No. 3. Later Bishop Henry Whipple came forward to defend the Ojibwas and, to a lesser extent, the Dakotas, from being banished from the state. On Whipple's role with the Ojibwas, see Martin N. Zanger, "'Straight Tongue's Heathen Wards': Bishop Whipple and the Episcopal Mission to the Chippewas," in *Churchmen and the Western Indians,* ed. Clyde A. Milner II and Floyd A. O'Neil (Norman: University of Oklahoma Press, 1985), 177–245.

80. Anderson, *Kinsmen;* Esther Wakeman's "Reminiscences" were given to her daughter decades after the event and published in 1960. They are important for, to the best of my knowledge, they are the only reminiscences of a Mdewakanton Dakota woman who went with Little Crow onto the plains

rather than of a Dakota or a partly Dakota Christian who identified with the U.S. cause. See Anderson and Woolworth, *Through Dakota Eyes*, 53–55.

81. The terms "crisis point" and "moral vantage point," as used here label categories of my own devising. See my earlier work: "Let me tell you something. Don't forget. Everything in your life *you decide* . . . unless they come with a gun at your head. . . . Even then you got a choice, either die or do what he says." From "Nicholas Gerros—Greek Horatio Alger," in June Namias, ed., *First Generation: In the Words of Twentieth-Century American Immigrants*, rev. ed., 2d ed. (Urbana: University of Illinois Press, 1992), 28.

82. Colonel H. H. Sibley wrote to his wife, Sarah Jane Steele Sibley, from near St. Peter in late August 1862, describing "poor people up here, who are being butchered by the score, with the horrible accompaniments of fearful mutilation." August 28, 1862, Sibley Papers, MHS.

83. Minnie Buce Carrigan, *Captured by the Indians: Reminiscences of a Pioneer Life in Minnesota* [Forest City, S.D., 1907], in *Narratives*, reprint vol. 106 (New York: Garland Publishing, 1977), 5–9.

84. Justina (Kitzman) Kreiger, "Narrative of Justina Kreiger," in *A History of the Great Massacre by the Sioux Indians, in Minnesota, Including the Personal Narratives of Many Who Escaped*, ed. Charles S. Bryant and Abel B. Murch (Cincinnati: Rickey & Carroll, 1864), 318–19, 323.

85. Ernestina Broburg, personal statement in Bryant and Murch, eds., *A History of the Great Massacre*, 401–3.

86. "Narrative of Justina Boelter," in Bryant and Murch, eds., *History of the Great Massacre*, 324–35.

87. Eastlick's story is seen by whites as the prototypical heroic story of a woman during the war. The mother of five children, Eastlick was one of the survivors of an incident near Lake Shetek in Murray County in southwestern Minnesota, a confrontation in which many whites died or were captured. The site came to be called "Slaughter Slough." Eastlick later lost another son, who died on the prairie. "Mrs. Eastlick and Family," in Bryant and Murch, eds., *History of the Great Massacre*, 78–82. For a melodramatic second-hand account years after the events, see H. J. Hibschman, *The Shetek Prisoners* (1901), Narratives, reprint vol. 104 (New York: Garland Publishing, 1976), 20–21.

88. Martha C. Nussbaum, *The Fragility of Goodness: Luck and Ethics in Greek Tragedy and Philosophy* (New York: Cambridge University Press, 1986), 1–3, 318–19.

89. Memorialized in Minnesota were the "good" Indians like Snana (Tinkling, or Maggie Brass), a Kaposia Mdewakanton who converted to Christianity and saved Mary Schwandt during the outbreak. See Anderson and Woolworth, eds., *Through Dakota Eyes*, 141–43, and Schwandt's account (listed in the bibliography's primary sources). For others, see Namias, *White Captives*, 242, 252. Also memorialized was John Otherday, who saved Dr. John Wakefield and other whites at the Upper Agency. The reverse stories—those of whites who protected Indians—are lost except for Sarah Wakefield's.

90. Helen M. Tarble, *The Story of My Capture and Escape during the Minnesota Indian Massacre of 1862* (St. Paul, 1904), 7–8.

91. Mary Schwandt, "Story of Mary Schwandt," 474; J. E. De Camp Sweet, "Mrs. J. E. De Camp Sweet's Narrative of Her Captivity in the Sioux Outbreak of 1862, *Minnesota Historical Society* Collections 6 (1896)," 354–56, 372.

92. Mrs. N. D. White [Urania Frazer], "Captivity among the Sioux, August 18 to September 26, 1862," *Minnesota Historical Society Collections* 9 (April 1901): 395–97, 426.

93. The few white men in Minnesota who came forward not at risk as Wakefield was. It can be argued that, as missionaries it was their job to help out; they had a Christian duty to protect their charges, the Indians. Bishop Whipple did lobby for the Ojibwas. Stephen Riggs and Thomas Williamson followed the banished Dakotas onto the high plains to effect more conversions. And Meyer argues that ministers like Samuel D. Hinman were beaten and other supportive ministers were at risk. Meyer, *History of Santee Sioux*), 138–39.

94. I was unable to gather much in the way of Wakefield's religious experience. Although she knew Rev. Thomas Williamson and participated in his church, I have no idea if she was an evangelical Christian or simply joined his church rather than Riggs's, which was the only other church in the territory. Her faith does not seem to me to be built on a conversion experience. Nor does she seem to dwell on "sin" or the depraved state of her soul. She seems altogether different from New England women discussed in Susan Juster's *Disorderly Women: Sexual Politics and Evangelicalism in Revolutionary New England* (Ithaca, N.Y.: Cornell University Press, 1994) and most of those discussed by Ann Douglas in *Feminization of American Culture*. On Dr. John Wakefield's role in treating the Dakota wounded, see, "The Battle between the Sioux and Chippewas at Shakopee," Shakopee *Weekly Pioneer and Democrat*, June 3, 1858.

95. Namias, *White Captives*, 257–60, and June Namias, "Race, Rape, and Mutual Motherhood: Sarah Wakefield Reading the Dakota War," paper presented at American Studies Association annual meeting, Boston, November 1993. Wakefield wondered why Williamson's mission was attacked. She liked the minister but realized something must have gone wrong in his relations with the Dakotas. Namias, *White Captives*, 242.

96. *Six Weeks* (1864), as reprinted here, p. 127.

97. When discussing captives who sympathize with their captors, people invariably bring up the Stockholm effect—the psychological phenomenon of identifying with one's captors. But this is hardly a *moral* position. My argument discounts that phenomenon, giving precedence to a moral choice. On womanhood and resistance in the autobiographies of this period, see Sidonie Smith's discussion of "unchaining the subject in chains" in her essay, "Elizabeth Cady Stanton, Harriet Jacobs, and Resistances to 'True Womanhood,'" in *Subjectivity, Identity, and the Body: Women's Autobiographical Practices in the Twentieth-Century* (Bloomington: University of Indiana Press, 1993), 24–52, esp. 50. For slave narratives that raise moral issues, see William L. Andrews,

"The Changing Moral Discourse of Nineteenth-Century African American Women's Autobiography: Harriet Jacobs and Elizabeth Keckley," in Smith and Watson, eds., *De Colonizing the Subject*, 225–41; and Jean Fagan Yellin, *Women and Sisters: The Antislavery Feminists in American Culture* (New Haven, Conn.: Yale University Press, 1989), 55, 31, 35.

98. The question concerning a New England heritage was raised by Daniel A. Cohen, and I myself raised it in comparing Wakefield with Harriet Beecher Stowe. See Namias, *White Captives*, 258–59.

99. Sara Ruddick, "Remarks on the Sexual Politics of Reason," in Kittay and Meyers, eds. *Women and Moral Theory*, 137–60, esp. 237, 254–55.

100. Micah 6:8, *The Holy Bible, Revised Standard Version*, ed. Herbert G. May and Bruce M. Metzger (New York: Oxford University Press, 1973), 1129.

Text of Six Weeks in the Sioux Tepees

1. The agency to which the Wakefields were assigned was variously called the Upper Sioux Agency, the Upper Agency, and Yellow Medicine. It was located north and west of Mankato, south and west of St. Paul along the Minnesota River at the juncture of the Yellow Medicine River, and thirty miles north and west of the Lower Sioux Agency (also called the Lower Agency or Redwood). At statehood in 1858 Minnesota became part of the Northern Superintendency. Joseph R. Brown, a Democrat, was appointed Minnesota's agent. With the election of the new Republican administration, Clark W. Thompson became the superintendent of Indian Affairs for the Northern Superintendency in 1861 and Thomas J. Galbraith of Shakopee was appointed agent to the Dakota Indians.

2. The gold was annuity money that was due in June. Annuity monies were promised twice a year to Dakotas as part of their treaties of 1851 and 1858. See Gary Clayton Anderson, *Kinsmen of Another Kind: Dakota-White Relations in the Upper Mississippi Valley, 1650–1862* (Lincoln: University of Nebraska Press, 1984), 248.

3. Joseph Reynolds and his wife were government school teachers who ran a boardinghouse. Anderson, *Kinsmen*, 265. Fort Ridgely was built in the early 1850s as part of the government's program to police the western frontier and to supervise reservation policy. It was built to implement the provisions of the treaty of 1851.

4. Indians in the nineteenth century commonly referred to the president as "the Great Father" and to heads of agencies as "Father." Father/son and father/child language was common. This familial language was often misinterpreted by whites as meaning that Indians consented to the paternal authority and patriarchal notions of the European heritage. Instead, for the Indian it reflected the notions of kinship in Native societies—that is, reciprocal relations rather than those handed down from an authority figure.

5. Between A.D. 700 and 1000 there was a surge of mound building in northern Georgia, which eventually swept north. Known as the Mississippian tradition, it produced many styles and "ritual centers that spread from the

upper Great Lakes to the lower Mississippi Valley." Peter Nabokov and Robert Easton, *Native American Architecture* (New York: Oxford University Press, 1989), 101.

6. John B. Renville was a Dakota-French who married Mary Butler, a white woman.

7. Dr. Rev. Thomas Smith Williamson (1800–79) was a Presbyterian missionary sent to Minnesota in 1835 by the American Board of Commissioners for Foreign Missions (ABCFM), headquartered in Boston. He organized the first Protestant church in Minnesota. He was graduated from Yale Medical College in 1824 and had practiced medicine before being ordained in 1834. In Minnesota he established three mission stations: at Little Crow's village, at Lac qui Parle, and at Yellow Medicine. In late 1852 he moved up the Minnesota River to build a mission at Pajutazee and the Dakota Church, both three miles north and west along the Minnesota River from the Upper Agency. Besides his mission work, Williamson translated the Bible into Dakota. Thomas S. Williamson Papers, in the American Board of Commissioners for Foreign Missions (hereafter ABCFM) collection at Houghton Library, Harvard University, Cambridge, Massachusetts. Used by permission ABCFM and the United Church Board for World Ministries. Also see Rev. S. R. Riggs, *A Memorial Discourse on Rev. Thomas S. Williamson, M.D., Mission to the Dakota Indians*, (New York: American Tract Society, n.d.), 15–17, in Jon Willand, *Lac qui Parle and the Dakota Mission*, (Madison, Minn.: n.p., 1964). See also Roy W. Meyer, *History of the Santee Sioux: United States Indian Policy on Trial* (Lincoln: University of Nebraska Press, 1967), 137–39, 96; and Warren Upham and Rose Barteau, comps., *Collections of the Minnesota Historical Society, Minnesota Biographies, 1655–1912* (hereafter *MB*) (St. Paul: Dunlap, 1912), 863.

8. The Dakota Church was the church founded by Williamson.

9. Reverend Stephen Return Riggs (1812–83) arrived in Minnesota as part of the ABCFM mission to the Dakotas in 1837. He built a mission at Hazelwood with his wife, Mary Riggs. Riggs wrote innumerable tracts on religion for the Dakotas along with translating the Bible, editing a Dakota-English dictionary, and writing autobiographical works of his experiences. See Stephen R. Riggs, *Tah-Koo Wah-Kan, or The Gospel among the Dakotas* (Boston: Congregational Sabbath-School and Publishing Society, 1869); Stephen R. Riggs, *Mary and I: Forty Years with the Sioux* (Chicago: W. G. Holmes, 1880); and the Stephen R. Riggs Papers, ABCFM.

10. The pipe and smoking have multiple functions in Dakota culture. Here the pleasure of smoking and the creation of stronger relationships appear to have been the intent. The sacred pipe is used in religious ceremonies of the Dakota and Lakota people. Catlinite, or red clay, pipes were characteristic of sacred pipes in southwestern Minnesota, the Pipestone Quarry in western Minnesota long being known as a sacred source for Dakota clay. See the Editor's Introduction to this text as well as Arval Looking Horse, "The Sacred Pipe in Modern Life" in *Sioux Indian Religion*, ed. Raymond J. DeMallie and Douglas R. Parks (Norman: University of Oklahoma Press, 1987), 67–73. Look-

ing Horse says, "Pipes made of this cherished red stone still play an important role among the Dakota." Also see Janet D. Spector, *What This Awl Means: Feminist Archeology at a Wahpeton Dakota Village* (St. Paul: Minnesota Historical Society Press, 1993), 114–16.

11. Major Thomas J. Galbraith was Lincoln's appointee as the Dakota agent in the Northern Superintendency. Major Joseph Renshaw Brown (1805–70) arrived in Minnesota at the age of fourteen and helped to build Fort Snelling. He became a fur trader, married Susan Frenier Brown, a French-Sisseton woman, and preceded Galbraith as Dakota agent. Brown was responsible for implementing the "civilization" clauses in the 1851 treaty, meaning that during his administration more schools were built, more land was cultivated, and the Upper Sioux Agency was built. However, he had a reputation for womanizing with young Dakota women. Meyer, *History of Santee Sioux*, 108; Anderson, *Kinsmen*, 141–42; Upham and Barteau, comps., *MB*, 84; and Louis H. Roddis, *The Indian Wars of Minnesota* (Cedar Rapids, Iowa: Torch Press, 1956), 204.

12. Mrs. G——h refers to Maj. Thomas Galbraith's wife, Henrietta (Garrison) Galbraith.

13. Sarah Wakefield was over six feet tall and weighed almost two hundred pounds.

14. The warehouse at the Yellow Medicine Agency was one of several buildings on the bluff above the river. For a discussion of the warehouse and a reconstruction of the Upper Agency, which was destroyed in the uprising, see the drawing by Chester Kozlak in Kenneth Carley, *The Sioux Uprising of 1862* (St. Paul: Minnesota Historical Society Press, 1976), 20; and "Location of Buildings at the Upper Agency, 1862," by George E. Olds, "Vicinity of the Upper Sioux Agency, 1862," in William Watts Folwell, *A History of Minnesota*, rev. ed., vol. 2 (St. Paul: Minnesota Historical Society Press, 1978), 116, 117.

The Wakefields' house was next to the agent's quarters and warehouse building. It contained five rooms—a parlor, "family room" (or bedroom), dining room, kitchen, and "help's room"—a storeroom, a closet, and an outhouse. See Sioux Claim of John L. Wakefield (hereafter J. L. Wakefield Sioux Claim), Sioux Uprising Collection Box 3, John L. Wakefield, Minnesota Historical Society (hereafter MHS).

15. Trading houses were very much a part of the system of government control of Indians in the nineteenth century before and during the Civil War. See the Editor's Introduction to the text.

16. The Dakotas were made up of four divisions: Sissetons, Wahpetons, Wahpekutes, and Mdewakantons. See the Editor's Introduction to the text.

17. These nine-dollar payments were to be distributed semiannually to each male member of the Dakotas who was enrolled and listed. This presumption of a male head of household was based on white American Protestant ideas and had implications for Dakota society, especially for those Dakota women who lost men in battle or to old age and for those younger women who were used by the traders and soldiers, bore children, and had no means to collect payments directly.

18. *Minne-wakan* means holy or sacred water.

19. There is some controversy over the use of the term "squaw." Deriving from the eastern Algonquian, in some circles it has evolved to slang, akin to "slut." Clearly Wakefield had no such intent here but simply used the word to mean an Indian woman.

20. The conflicts between Ojibwas (or Chippewas) and Eastern Dakotas dated back a century.

21. Reverend Samuel D. Hinman was an Episcopalian minister. He was later active in baptizing some of the Dakotas taken prisoner in the wake of the outbreak.

22. Acton was the township where four young Mdewakanton men first challenged and then shot a white farmer, two other white men, a woman, and a girl on Sunday, August 17, around noon. Folwell, *History of Minnesota*, vol. 2, 239.

23. George Gleason ran the steamer *Frank Steel*, or *Favorite*, from 1858 to 1860. With Galbraith's appointment as Indian agent, Gleason was chosen as a clerk at the Redwood (or Lower) Agency.

24. Stewart P. Garvie was a trader at the Upper Agency. The Big Woods was a favorite Dakota hunting ground, especially before statehood.

25. Among the Dakota, the name Chaska was given to all first-born sons.

26. Among the Dakota, the name Hapa was given to all second-born sons.

27. Rice Creek was about halfway between the two agencies and close to Shakopee's village along the Minnesota River. The villages of Shakopee and Red Middle Voice were Rice Creek Indian villages. In some writings, "Rice Creek Indian" is synonymous with Shakopee's band.

28. Shakopee (pronounced Shock'-o-pee) was built on the site of the Mdewakanton village of Shu'k pay (also Shakpay, Shakopee, Shanaydan, or Little Six). Today it is less than a one-hour drive south and west of the Twin Cities. In 1847, Shakopee allowed Rev. Samuel W. Pond to set up a school, a mission, and a gristmill in the village. Two years after the treaty of Traverse des Sioux (1851), 350 members of the Shakopee band left this site for Shakopee's village along the Minnesota River near Redwood (the Lower Agency). The number 350 was suggested by Alan R. Woolworth, comment to the editor, February 8, 1995.

29. On May 27, 1858, there was a battle between the Dakotas and the Ojibwas in the Shakopee area, in Scott County south and west of St. Paul. After the battle, Dr. John Wakefield treated Dakota wounded. "The Battle between the Sioux and Chippewas at Shakopee," Shakopee *Weekly Pioneer and Democrat*, June 3, 1858; Shakopee *Daily Minnesotan*, July 1, 1858; Shakopee *Daily Minnesotan*, December 21, 1857. These papers are in the collections of the Minnesota Historical Society.

30. Tepees were used when Dakotas traveled or hunted. They were made from buffalo hides and were put up rapidly with fifteen-foot saplings. A smoke hole was left for the fire to escape. In the winter months dry swamp grasses were picked by women to bank on the floors and walls of the tepee for warmth. In the summer, bark houses were built. Gary Clayton Anderson, *Little Crow:*

Spokesman for the Sioux (St. Paul: Minnesota Historical Society Press, 1986), 13. For contemporary drawings of the summer and winter housing of the Dakotas, see Bertha I. Heilbron, ed., *With Pen and Pencil on the Frontier in 1851: The Diary and Sketches of Frank Blackwell Mayer* (St. Paul: Minnesota Historical Society Press, 1986), 111–12, and the various sketches of Seth Eastman.

31. Meat, usually buffalo meat, was dried in the sun and then pounded with a maul. It was "mixed with melted fat, marrow, and the dry paste from wild cherries that had been crushed, pits and all." Robert H. Lowie, *Indians of the Plains* (Garden City, N.Y.: American Museum of Natural History Press, 1963), 27. Called pemmican, this dried meat was stored in parfleche (leather) bags. It was widely used by Plains Indians.

32. Northern and central European immigrants prized their feather beds. Many immigrants had carted them to ports and brought them on shipboard and then across the continent. The comforters were probably deeply symbolic as well, connecting one to childhood, sleep, and comfort.

33. Women of this era often wore hoops of whalebone or other flexible materials under their petticoats to expand the size of dresses or skirts.

34. Sissetons, or Upper Indians, were Dakota-speaking. They occupied villages on the upper portion of the Minnesota River along Big Stone Lake and along the Blue Earth River. There was much intermarriage between different Dakota bands and there was also intermarriage with the French. Sissetons were the largest of the Eastern Dakotas, numbering over two thousand of the four thousand Eastern Dakotas. Anderson, *Little Crow*, 11. Many opposed involvement in the war.

35. Early morning on August 19 John Otherday guided Dr. Wakefield and sixty-one other refugees from Yellow Medicine, along with others from the Riggs and Williamson missions, to safety. They crossed the Minnesota River and continued across the prairie to Cedar City, Shakopee, St. Paul, and other towns. They were photographed on August 21 by Adrian J. Ebell. Carley, *Sioux Uprising*, 19. See photo herein, p. 88, "MHS Collections: Adrian J. Ebell, Photographer and Journalist of the Dakota War of 1862," *Minnesota History* 52, 2 (Summer, 1994): 87–92.

36. Winona was Hapa's wife and Chaska's sister. Winona in Dakota means first daughter and is a common Dakota name.

37. A sacque is a loose gown.

38. George Spencer (1821–92) traded with Dakotas at Big Stone Lake after 1860. By 1862 he was a clerk at the Lower Agency. He was one of the few white men captured in the war who survived in the camp of Little Crow. He was wounded on August 18 at the Lower Agency but was saved by a Dakota by the name of Chaska (no relation to the Chaska who saved the Wakefields). Spencer wrote an account of his capture. In it he claimed that although he was treated well, "the female captives were, with very few exceptions, subjected to the most horrible treatment. In some cases a woman would be taken into the woods and her person violated by 6, 7, and as many as 10 or 12 of these fiends at one time." The Sioux Commission, 1863, National Archives Record Group 48,

entry no. 663. George H. Spencer, Jr., 1862, 15. Whether Spencer was telling the truth or using the language of the mass rape hysteria that inflamed political discussion of the uprising is hard to know. There is no other verification of any such wide use of rape during the war. Also see William Watts Folwell, *The Court Proceedings in the Trial of Dakota Indians Following the Massacre in Minnesota in August 1862* (Minneapolis: Satterlee Printing, 1927), 9–11, and Upham and Barteau, comps., MB, 727.

39. Kinnikinnick is Dakota tobacco made with both tobacco and alder bark. Reverend Samuel Pond mentions ceremonial use of tobacco in *The Dakota or Sioux in Minnesota as They Were in 1834* [1908], introduction by Gary Clayton Anderson (St. Paul: Minnesota Historical Society Press, 1986), 89, 122. For a contemporary but controversial discussion of the sacred pipe and White Buffalo Calf Woman, see Wallace H. Black Elk and William S. Lyons, *Black Elk: The Sacred Ways of a Lakota* (New York: Harper San Francisco, 1991), 53.

40. "Pa Baska," or *p' baska* or "cut head," is also the name of a Sioux group. Note by Raymond DeMallie to the editor, May 1996.

41. According to Samuel Pond, Eagle's Head, or Ruyapa, had murdered a woman in Shakopee and moved to Eagle Creek (in Scott County) where with "his relatives and others around him, he finally became a chief." Pond, *Dakota*, 8. The village of Ruyapa or Eagle's Head, is a Dakota village mentioned in Edmund C. Bray and Martha Coleman Bray, trans. and eds., *Joseph N. Nicollet on the Plains and Prairies: The Expeditions of 1838–39, With Journals, Letters, and Notes on the Dakota Indians* (St. Paul: Minnesota Historical Society Press, 1993], 44, 257.

42. "Far worse than death" and "a fate worse than death" were nineteenth-century code words for rape.

43. According to Raymond DeMallie, "'talk with you,' said by a Dakota man to a woman, would indicate a sexual relationship." Note to the editor, fall 1995.

44. Before death, Plains Indians dressed a person in their best clothes. See Lowie, *Indians of the Plains,* 89. Captivity narratives sometimes allude to the significance of clothing in matters of life and death. Mary Jemison's mother knew her daughter would live and she would die because Mary had been given new moccasins. James E. Seaver, *A Narrative of the Life of Mrs. Mary Jemison* [1824], ed. June Namias (Norman: University of Oklahoma Press, 1992), 69.

45. Little Crow (Taoyateduta, or His Red Nation) was the Mdewakanton leader who became the reluctant key figure in the war. He died on July 3, 1863. See Anderson, *Little Crow.*

46. Shakopee the elder (also called Little Six) was important in the earlier negotiations of the Minnesota treaties. A leading figure among the Mdewakanton, he died in 1857. He was followed by his son Shakopee, who was often also called Little Six. Wakefield's reference here is to the younger Shakopee.

47. Other examples of Christian Indian rescuers exist. Lorenzo Lawrence was one of Rev. Thomas S. Williamson's first Christian Indian converts. Lorenzo and Simon, both elders from Riggs's church, helped white settlers es-

cape the first days of the uprising. See J. E. De Camp Sweet, "Mrs. J. E. De Camp Sweet's Narrative of Her Captivity in the Sioux Outbreak of 1862," *Minnesota Historical Society Collections* 6 (1894)," 371–78. "Paul" refers to Paul Mazakutemani, or Mosm-coota-Moni (He Who Shoots as He Walks), a Wahpeton who was an early convert and friend to Stephen R. Riggs. He is said to have rescued Abbie Gardner during the Spirit Lake massacre in Iowa in 1856. Upham and Barteau, comps., *MB.* Also see Gary Clayton Anderson and Alan R. Woolworth, eds., *Through Dakota Eyes: Narrative Accounts of the Minnesota Indian War of 1862* (St. Paul: Minnesota Historical Society Press, 1988), 445.

48. Jane Williamson was the sister of Rev. Thomas S. Williamson.

49. Although summer heat in Minnesota is intense, head coverings were unusual among Dakotas. "In the sign language, a White man is indicated by drawing the right hand across the forehead to suggest a hat, a fact that implies the absence of native headgear in ordinary circumstances." Lowie, *Indians of the Plains,* 52. Although Indians wore fur hats in the winter and rawhide visors protected their eyes from the summer sun, the norm was no hat.

50. The travois was commonly used by north central and Plains groups. Two long poles extending out in a V shape were attached, one on either side, to a dog or horse. Bundles were placed on top of some form of woven reed or leather support strung between the poles. Women were usually in charge of packing the travois. See Lowie, *Indians of the Plains,* 40–42.

51. Another captive, Jannette Sykes De Camp, notes that during their capture and travels upriver with the Dakotas they passed the body of George Gleason. She had known him before coming to Redwood. "Mrs. J. E. De Camp Sweet's Narrative," 368.

52. The "soldiers' lodge" was a institution that had to do with hunting and communal responsibilities as well as warfare. The lodges often served as councils. Anderson, *Little Crow,* 41, 81–82.

53. Chief Akepa, or Joseph Akipa Renville, and his family were related to Maj. Joseph R. Brown, Indian agent before Galbraith.

54. John Otherday (Other Day) (Ampatutokacha, or Good Sounding Voice) guided Dr. Wakefield and others in escaping from the Upper Agency. (See note 35.)

55. Good Thunder, or Andrew (Wakinyanwaste or Wakeah Washta), and his wife, Snana (Tinkling, or Maggie Brass), were Christian. She was educated at Dr. Williamson's mission school. They married when she was about fifteen years old and in 1861 became the first Dakota couple to join the Presbyterian mission church. Snana saved the life of Mary Schwandt, a German captive. See "The Story of Mary Schwandt. Her Captivity during the Sioux 'Outbreak,'— 1862." *Minnesota Historical Society Collections* 6 (1896), and "Narrative of Mary Schwandt," in Charles S. Bryant and Able B. Murch, *A History of the Great Massacre by the Sioux Indians, in Minnesota, Including the Personal Narratives of Many Who Escaped* (Cincinnati: Rickey & Carroll, 1864), 335–42. On multiple editions, see June Namias, "White Captives: Gender and Ethnicity on Successive American Frontiers, 1607–1862," Ph.D. diss., Brandeis University, 1988, 548. For

her Snana's own account and further biographical information, see "Snana's Story," in Anderson and Woolworth, *Through Dakota Eyes*, 141–43, 257–58.

56. Julia Laframbois (also spelled LaFramboise and LaFrambois) was from a Dakota-French family. She was part Sisseton. Her father, Joseph LaFramboise, was the son of a Dakota woman and a French fur trader. Her family lived near the Upper Agency in 1862. Folwell, *History of Minnesota*, vol. 2, 426–27; and Anderson and Woolworth, *Through Dakota Eyes*, 108–12.

57. Cut Nose was a member of Little Crow's band. Jannette De Camp claims he tried to kill her when the party was north of New Ulm near where the Reynoldses lived and that he "had sworn to kill every man, woman and child he was able to kill." De Camp Sweet, "Mrs. J. E. De Camp Sweet's Narrative," 367.

58. Birch Coolie (or Birch Coulee) was a major battle of the uprising. It took place on September 2 before dawn, when Gray Bird, one of Little Crow's warriors, along with about 350 Dakotas attacked Minnesota men under the command of Capt. Joseph Anderson and Maj. Joseph R. Brown (former Indian agent in Minnesota). Thirteen Minnesota men and some 90 horses were killed that day. Close to 50 men were wounded, some of them dying later. It was the worst defeat of the revolt for U.S. forces. Subsequently, Colonel Silbey sent 240 men from Fort Ridgley to the rescue. Carley, *Sioux Uprising*, 40–44; and Folwell, *History of Minnesota*, vol. 2, 151–54.

59. Jannette E. Sykes De Camp Sweet (b. 1833) wrote her narrative on March 14, 1894, more than thirty years after the events. Her family line had originated in England, her ancestors coming to Minnesota via New England and New York State, where she had been born. She had married Joseph Warren De Camp who she claimed was descended from Gen. Joseph Warren who had fought at Bunker Hill. Married in Ohio in 1852, the couple had come to Minnesota in 1855, settling in Shakopee and living there until they moved to the Redwood Agency when her husband was appointed by Galbraith as head of the sawmill. Since Shakopee was such a small town and Galbraith's circle there was not large, it is highly likely that Jannette De Camp and Sarah Wakefield knew each other before their capture. De Camp's second husband was Rev. Joshua Sweet, chaplain at Fort Ridgely. See "Mrs. J. E. De Camp Sweet's Narrative," 354–80, 378; Upham and Barteau, comps., Sweet, in *MB*, 761–62; Julius A. Collier II, *The Shakopee Story* (Shakopee, Minn.: Lakewood Press, 1960); and Namias, "White Captives," 338–39.

60. Before substantial European contact, Native women's clothing was made of dressed skins. After contact, however, Native women found trade cloth easier to sew and equally warm. Wool trade cloth, especially in blue, black, and red, was common in Indian country from the early days of the fur trade. Often calico took the place of skins in summer. Decoration could include animal teeth or beads. For dress of the Plains groups, see Lowie, *Indians of the Plains*, 49–51.

61. Miss E. B—— is Ellen Brown, the daughter of Joseph R. Brown, former Dakota agent in Minnesota, and Susan Frenier Brown, a French-Dakota woman. Ellen was twenty years old when she was captured. Susan Frenier

Brown was able to save most of her family from capture. According to an account by her son, Samuel J. Brown, who was then seventeen, his mother and five or six neighboring families left their homes in Renville County at four in the afternoon on August 18. They were eight miles south of the Upper Agency and mistakenly, like Wakefield and her children, headed toward Fort Ridgely. When a group of hostile and rebelling Dakotas surrounded the group, Susan Brown "stood up in the wagon, waved her shawl and cried in a loud voice, in the Dakotah language, that she was a Sisseton and a relative of Wannaton, Scarlet Plume, Sweet Corn, and Ah-Kee-Pah, and the friend of Standing Buffalo, and that she expected protection." At that point, one of the Dakotas, who had been saved from freezing the previous winter by Susan Brown's mother, recognized her and jumped into the wagon to testify on her behalf. Mrs. Brown also threatened vengeance by Sissetons and Wahpetons upon the Mdewakantons. George G. Allanson, *The Stirring Adventures of the Joseph R. Brown Family* [1899], in *Narratives of North American Indian Captivity* (1899) (hereafter *Narratives*), reprint, vol. 103 (New York: Garland Publishing, 1976), first eight pages. Also see account by Samuel J. Brown to the 56th Congress, 2nd Session, Doc. No. 23, December 5, 1900, 1–36.

62. The pot is probably seen as taboo after a woman holds it. Menstrual taboos were strong among many Native peoples. Menstrual blood was seen as having sacred powers. Thus a woman of childbearing age held in her hands the power over life and death. Rayna Green, *Native American Women: A Contextual Bibliography* (Bloomington: University of Indiana Press, 1983) and Lowie, *Plains Indians,* 88–90, 184.

63. Medicine bags or medicine bundles are sacred objects among the Dakota and many other Plains Indians. When Little Crow died, he passed his medicine bundle to his son. See Anderson, *Little Crow,* 20, 91, 177.

64. Red Iron (Mazasha) was chief of an Upper Sioux village near Camp Release.

65. Lac qui Parle is at the junction of the Lac qui Parle and Minnesota Rivers in Minnesota north and west of the Upper Agency. It was an important fur trading and French-Dakota village. Gary C. Anderson, "Joseph Renville and the Ethos of Biculturalism," in *Being and Becoming Indian: Biographical Studies of North American Frontiers,* ed. James A. Clifton (Chicago: Dorsey Press, 1989), 59–81.

66. Thomas A. Robertson was an interpreter.

67. Ma a ha, or Mazasha, meant red iron, copper, or a penny.

68. Wakefield accepted the belief of many whites of her era that Indians really had no religion, but believed in "superstitions" and could only be "saved" by becoming Christian.

69. There were both sacred and secular dances among American Native groups in the nineteenth century as there are today. Whites tended to interpret these as "wild" and otherwise meaningless events. In fact, the dances served many functions in Native society. Although seen through missionary eyes, an account of the Dakota medicine dance may be found in Pond, *Dakota,* 95.

70. Standing Buffalo was one of the Sisseton chiefs who, like Red Iron, had opposed Little Crow and the Mdewakanton's decision to go to war. See Anderson, *Little Crow,* 155.

71. The Renvilles formed a large extended family. Mary Butler Renville was captured from S. R. Riggs's Hazelwood mission and later wrote a narrative of her experiences: *A Thrilling Narrative of Indian Captivity* (Minneapolis: Atlas Company's Books and Job Office, 1863).

72. A rod is equivalent to 5 1/2 yards or 16 1/2 feet; three rods thus represents approximately 50 feet.

73. Maz-coota-Meni was Paul Mazakutemani (He Who Shoots as He Walks), or Little Paul.

74. Wabasha was a significant leader of the Eastern Dakotas. His band was located in the village of the same name, to the east of the Lower Agency. Wacota (also Wakute or Wacouta) was chief of the Red Wing Dakota band.

75. Colonel Henry Hastings Sibley (1811–91), an early settler in Minnesota Territory, was a fur trader in the 1830s and 1840s. He later became a state legislator, newspaper owner, and, eventually, governor of Minnesota. During the Dakota War he was appointed head of the captive rescue mission and in the process rose in rank from colonel to general. June Namias, *White Captives: Gender and Ethnicity on the American Frontier* (Chapel Hill: University of North Carolina Press, 1993), 219.

76. Antonine Joseph Campbell, his wife, Mary, and their family were "mixed-bloods" who were taken captive. The account of their daughter, Cecilia (Celia) Campbell Stay, can be found in Anderson and Woolworth, eds., *Through Dakota Eyes,* 44–52.

77. Mrs. Dr. Humphrey was Susan Angier (Ames) Humphrey, the wife of Philander P. Humphrey, a physician at the Lower Agency. She was killed on August 18, 1862, fleeing to Fort Ridgely. The physician and his wife were both born in Connecticut and moved to Minnesota in 1852. John Ames Humphrey, "Boyhood Remembrances of Life among the Dakotas and the Massacre in 1862," *Collections of the Minnesota Historical Society* 15 (May 1915): 22; notes from Alan Woolworth of the Minnesota Historical Society.

78. Camp Release was so named by the U.S. military because it was here on the upper Minnesota River, south of Lac qui Parle, that the white and mixed-blood captives were handed over to the army.

79. Hutchinson, Minnesota, is in McLeod County, west of the Twin Cities and north of New Ulm.

80. Mrs. A—— may well be a Mrs. Adams. If so, she is referred to by Mary Schwandt as being, with Wakefield, too friendly with the Dakotas. She may also be the woman referred to by Sibley in a letter to his wife, Sarah Steele Sibley, in which he discussed a woman who was sleeping with an Indian lover: "one rather handsome woman" who "had become so infatuated with the red skin who had taken her for his wife, that, although her white husband was still living at some point below, and had been in search of her, she declared that were it not for her children, she would not leave her dusky paramour." Henry

Hastings Sibley Papers, 1815–1930, Minnesota Historical Society, microfilm, September 27, 1862. It should be pointed out here that there is some chance this reference is to Wakefield herself. See Namias, *White Captives*, chap. 6; Schwandt, "Story of Mary Schwandt," 472–73.

81. Between September 28 and November 5, a military commission was organized to try Dakotas who had participated in the outbreak. It was composed of Col. William Crooks (1832–1907) of the Sixth Regiment of Minnesota Infantry, Lt. Col. William R. Marshall (1825–96) of the Seventh, Capt. Hiram P. Grant (1828–97) of the sixth, Capt. Hiram S. Bailey (dates not found) of the sixth, and 1st Lt. Rollin C. Olin (dates not found) of the third. The judge advocate was Isaac V. D. Heard (1834–1913) a lawyer. In 1861, Marshall had founded the *St. Paul Press*, the major Republican paper of the state. He later served in the Civil War, becoming a brigadier general in 1865. Heard became a state senator in 1871. Upham and Barteau, comps., *MB*, 490.

82. "Capt. Grant" is Capt. Hiram P. Grant.

83. This is a reference to "Godfrey, a Negro," as he was called in the records. He was one of the original thirty-nine condemned to hang, but was let off at the last minute for his role as a witness against other Indians. See Namias, *White Captives*, 232–33.

84. During the first day of the uprising, a Dakota named Chaska, or Wakinyantawa, saved Spencer. See note 38.

85. Major William J. Cullen, superintendent of Indian Affairs.

86. Wood Lake was close to but south of the Upper Agency. After the battle fought there on September 23 against H. H. Sibley, some Dakotas made the decision to leave for the plains. Anderson and Woolworth, *Through Dakota Eyes*, 15. On the battle of Wood Lake, see Folwell, *History of Minnesota*, vol. 2, 178–82, passim.

87. John Mooers was the son of Hazen P. Mooers, a trader, and Mahpiya Hotawin, or Gray Cloud. See Pond, *Dakota*, 115–17. "Capt. McClarthy" is possibly Robert McLaren (b. 1828) who raised a company for the sixth Minnesota Regiment. Alan Woolworth, note to the editor, February 8, 1995.

88. Captain John Kennedy was born in Ontario. He enlisted in the Seventh Minnesota Regiment in 1862 and became a brevet major. Upham and Barteau, comps., *MB*, 397.

89. One newspaper listed Chaska as no. 20, Chas-kay-dan, the savior of "Mrs. Wakefield and her children." "Confession of the Prisoners," *Saint Paul Daily Press*, December 28, 1862. On the original trial listings that went to Lincoln there were several Chaska name look-alikes: Chaskay-Don, or Chaskay-Eteh, no. 121; Chayton-Hoon-Ka, no. 342; Chan-Ka-Hda, no. 359. Found in *Message of the President of the United States in Answer to the Resolution of the Senate of the 5th Instant in Relation to the Indian Barbarities in Minnesota, December 11, 1862*, in Records of the Trial of Sioux-Dakota Indians in Minnesota, 1862. NA Record Group 4, 37th Congress, 3d session, Records of the Military Commission that tried Sioux-Dakota Indians for barbarities committed in Minnesota, 1862, D, 5–6. See president's list, p. 34 herein.

90. We-chan-hpe-was-tay-do-pee was Chaska's Dakota name. Reverend S. R. Riggs spelled the name We-chan-hpe-wash-tay-do-pe in his letter to Sarah Wakefield. Between the cover page and the rest of the trial records there are five spellings of Chaska's name: We-Chank-Wash-ta-don-pee; We-chank-wash-tah-dow-pee; We=chank=wash, tu da pee; We=chank=to=do=pee; and We-chank-wash-tu-do-pe.

91. Chaskay, a Christian Indian prisoner who had been part of Riggs's church at Hazelwood near Yellow Medicine, had been renamed Robert Hopkins. He organized prayer meetings in the Mankato prison the week before the hanging. His work paved the way for Riggs, Williamson, Rev. Gideon H. Pond, and others to baptize three hundred Dakota men. See Rev. T. S. Williamson to S. B. Treat at ABCFM, April 10, 1863, Williamson Papers, ABCFM; Folwell, *History of Minnesota*, vol. 2, 250–51; Riggs, *Memorial Discourse*, 15–17. On the trial and execution, see Namias, *White Captives*, 219–37.

92. Amanda M. Macomber Earle was one of three women held by Little Crow. My guess is that Julia Earle was the young captive. See Samuel J. Brown's account to Congress, December 5, 1900, 1–36.

93. Wakefield refers to the Indian expedition of Gen. H. H. Sibley against the Sioux who had moved into Dakota Territory in June and July 1863. This indicates that this part of the narrative by Wakefield was written in or after the summer months of 1863.

94. Dr. Josiah S. Weiser was a surgeon and a member of the Minnesota Mounted Rangers.

95. Alfred Sully (1821–79) served in the Mexican War and was a colonel in the third Minnesota Regiment in 1862. In 1863–64 he led expeditions into the Dakota Territory in search of the Dakotas who had fled with Little Crow.

96. By 1862 the Winnebagos, like the Dakotas, were destitute, with little game or food. Both General Sibley and General Pope were instrumental in the deportation of the Winnebagoes, claiming that these Indians too were instrumental in the outbreak. Some Winnebagos were even among the close to four hundred Natives tried at Camp Release, but none was among those hanged. An act of Congress was passed on February 21, 1863, requiring the removal of the Winnebagos to land beyond any state, but suitable for agriculture. Superintendent Clark W. Thompson selected the new Winnebago lands and organized the group's removal to Dakota Territory on the Missouri River. In all, 1,945 Winnebagos were "removed," including 531 men and 1,414 women and children. They were moved again in March of 1865, this time to northeast Nebraska. Warren Upham, *Aborigines of Minnesota*, Collections of the Minnesota Historical Society (St. Paul: Dunlap, 1912) 573–74.

97. Brules and Tetons are Lakotas, or Plains Sioux.

SELECTED BIBLIOGRAPHY

GENERAL REFERENCES

For bibliography on the Dakotas, see Herbert T. Hoover, *The Sioux: A Critical Bibliography* (Bloomington: University of Indiana Press, 1979), compiled for the Newberry Library Center for the History of the American Indian; Herbert T. Hoover and Karen P. Zimmerman, comps., *The Sioux and Other Native American Cultures in the Dakotas: An Annotated Bibliography* (Westport, Conn.: Greenwood Press, 1993); Jack W. Marken and Herbert T. Hoover, *Bibliography of the Sioux* (Metuchen, N.J.: Scarecrow Press, 1980). On Indian bibliography, see Francis Paul Prucha, *Indian-White Relations in the United States: A Bibliography of Works Published, 1975–1980* (Lincoln: University of Nebraska Press, 1982). On captivity narratives, see Alden T. Vaughan, ed., *Narratives of North American Indian Captivity: A Selective Bibliography* (New York: Garland Publishing, 1983), with an introduction by Wilcomb E. Washburn. Also see the 110 other volumes in this series of reprints of captivity narratives, including many from Minnesota. For other captivity experiences of Minnesota women, see the primary sources section that follows and the endnotes to the Editor's Introduction. For the most complete reference work on American Indians, see William C. Sturtevant, gen. ed., *Handbook of North American Indians,* especially Wilcomb E. Washburn, vol. ed., *History of Indian-White Relations,* vol. 4 (Washington, D.C.: Smithsonian Institution, 1988) and *Plains,* forthcoming. On Native autobiography, see H. David Brumble III, *An Annotated Bibliography of American Indian and Eskimo Autobiographies* (Lincoln: University of Nebraska Press, 1981), and Arnold Krupat, ed., *Native American Autobiography: An Anthology* (Madison: University of Wisconsin, 1994). On Native women, see Rayna Green, *Native American Women: A Contextual Bibliography* (Bloomington: University of Indiana Press, 1983). On Indian law, see Charles J.

Kappler, comp., *Indian Affairs: Laws and Treaties*, vol. II (Washington, D.C.: U.S. Government Printing Office, 1904), and most recent editions. On women's writing, see Cathy N. Davidson, *Revolution and the Word: The Rise of the Novel in America* (New York: Oxford University Press, 1986).

PRIMARY SOURCES

There are two editions of Sarah Wakefield's narrative: The first is Mrs. Sarah F. Wakefield, *Six Weeks in the Sioux Tepees: A Narrative of Indian Captivity* (Minneapolis: Atlas Printing, 1863), found in microform in *Western Americana: Frontier History of the Trans-Mississippi West, 1550–1900*, reel 586, no. 6042. The only known copy is in the Western Americana Collection of the Beinecke Library, Yale University. The second is Mrs. Sarah F. Wakefield, *Six Weeks in the Sioux Tepees: A Narrative of Indian Captivity* (Shakopee, Minn.: Argus Book and Job Printing Office, 1864), the text of which is the basis for this edition. See *Narratives of North American Indian Captivity*, reprint vol. 79 (New York: Garland Publishing, 1977).

The Minnesota Historical Society, Saint Paul, Minnesota, and its Division of Manuscripts has the largest collections of documents and books on Minnesota history. Their material relating to the Wakefields includes the deposition of J. L. Wakefield in the Sioux Uprising Collection; the Alexander Ramsey Papers, 1815–1903 (microfilm); the Henry Hastings Sibley Papers (microfilm); and the Scott County files and newspapers taken from the Writers' Project Annals, Scott County, Minnesota, 1852–1869. They also have one of the few original copies of *Six Weeks in the Sioux Tepees: A Narrative of Indian Captivity* (1864). Data on the births and residences of the Wakefields may be found in the Minnesota census records for Scott and Ramsey Counties. Marriage and probate records may be found in the Scott County Court House, Shakopee, Minnesota. Other primary and government documents on the Wakefield family may be found at the Blue Earth County Historical Society, Mankato, Minnesota; the Faribault County Historical Society, Blue Earth, Minnesota; and the J. B. Wakefield House Museum, Blue Earth, Minnesota.

The National Archives, Washington, D.C., has records of the military commission that tried the Dakota Indians, including Sarah Wakefield's testimony on behalf of Chaska, or We-Chank-wash-ta-don-pee. These records are also available on microfilm from the National Archives.

For an excellent library of American Indian materials visit the Newberry Library, Chicago. See *Dictionary Catalogue of the Edward E. Ayer Collection of Americana and American Indians in the Newberry Library* (Boston: G. K. Hall, 1961) and *First Supplement* (Boston: G. K. Hall, 1970). The Newberry also has the best collection of original captivity narratives from all eras.

Letters and other materials from Stephen R. Riggs and Thomas Williamson, two prominent ministers on the Minnesota frontier, are to be found in the

American Board of Commissioners for Foreign Missions Papers at Houghton Library, Harvard University, Cambridge, Massachusetts.

Minnesota newspapers of the period include Faribault *Central Republican*, Shakopee *Daily Minnesotan, Mankato Daily Free Press,* Shakopee *Weekly Pioneer and Democrat,* St. Paul *Pioneer and Democrat, St. Paul Daily Pioneer, Shakopee Argus, Mankato Independent, and St. Paul Daily Pioneer.*

Printed collections of Dakota viewpoints of the Dakota War include Gary Clayton Anderson and Alan R. Woolworth, eds., *Through Dakota Eyes: Narrative Accounts of the Minnesota Indian War of 1862* (St. Paul: Minnesota Historical Society Press, 1988).

PRIMARY DOCUMENTS AND EARLY REFERENCE BOOKS
OF MINNESOTA HISTORY INCLUDE:

Allanson, George C. The *Stirring Adventures of the Joseph R. Brown Family* [1899]. *In Narratives of North American Indian Captivity* (hereafter *Narratives*). Reprint vol. 103. New York: Garland Publishing, 1976.

Bishop, Harriet. *Floral Home: or First Years of Minnesota.* In *Chronology and Documentary Handbook of the State of Minnesota.* Edited by Robert I. Vexler and William F. Swindler [1857]. Reprinted. Dobbs Ferry, N.Y.: Oceana, 1978.

Board of Commissioners. *Minnesota in the Civil and Indian Wars, 1861–1865.* St. Paul: Pioneer Press, 1890.

Bowen, Ralph H., ed. and trans. *A Frontier Family in Minnesota: Letters of Theodore and Sophie Bost, 1815–1920.* Minneapolis: University of Minnesota Press, 1981.

Bryant, Charles S., and Abel B. Murch. *A History of the Great Massacre by the Sioux Indians, in Minnesota, Including the Personal Narratives of Many Who Escaped.* Cincinnati: Rickey & Carroll, 1864.

Carrigan, Minnie Buce. Captured by the Indians: Reminiscences of Pioneer Life in Minnesota. [1907, 1912]. In *Narratives.* Reprint vol. 106. New York: Garland Publishing, 1977.

Carrothers Helen M. Paddock, [Mrs. Helen M. Tarble]. *The Story of My Capture and Escape during the Minnesota Indian Massacre of 1862* [1904]. In *Narratives.* Reprint vol. 105. New York: Garland Publishing, 1976.

"Chief Big Eagle's Story of the Sioux Outbreak of 1862" [Wamditanka]. *Minnesota Historical Society Collections* 6 (1894): 382–401.

Connolly, A. P. *A Thrilling Narrative of the Minnesota Massacre and the Sioux War of 1862–63.* Chicago: A. P. Connolly, 1896.

De Camp Sweet, J. E. "Mrs. J. E. De Camp Sweet's Narrative of Her Captivity in the Sioux Outbreak of 1862." *Minnesota Historical Society Collections* 6 (1894): 354–80.

Deloria, Ella. *Dakota Texts.* Volume XIV, *Publications of the American Ethnological Society.* Edited by Franz Boas. New York: G. E. Stechert, 1932.

Eastman, Charles [Ohiyesa]. *From the Deep Woods to Civilization.* Boston: Little Brown, 1916.

————. *Indian Boyhood.* 1902. Williamstown, Mass.: Corner House Publishers, 1975.

————. *The Soul of the Indian: An Interpretation.* 1911. Reprinted. Lincoln: University of Nebraska Press, 1980.

Eastman, Mrs. Mary [Henderson]. *Dahcotah, or Life and Legends of the Sioux around Fort Snelling.* New York: John Wiley, 1849.

Folwell, William Watts. *A History of Minnesota* [1924]. 4 vols. Revised ed. St. Paul: Minnesota Historical Society Press, 1978.

Heard, Isaac V. D. *History of the Sioux War and Massacres of 1862 and 1863* [1864]. Reprinted. Milwood, N.Y.: Krause Reprint, 1975.

Huggan, Nancy McClure Faribault. "The Story of Nancy McClure." *Minnesota Historical Society Collections* 6(1894): 439–60.

Juni, Benedict. *Held in Captivity: Benedict Juni, of New Ulm, Minn. Relates His Experience as an Indian Captive during the Indian Outbreak in 1862* [1926]. Reprinted. New Ulm, Minn.: Lowell F. Juni, 1977.

Kelly, Fanny. *My Captivity among the Sioux Indians.* 3d ed. Chicago: R. R. Donnelley & Sons, 1891.

Mayer, Frank Blackwell. *With Pen and Pencil on the Frontier in 1851: The Diary and Sketches of Frank Blackwell Mayer.* Edited by Bertha I. Heilbron. St. Paul: Minnesota Historical Society Press, 1986.

McConkey, Harriet E. Bishop. *Dakota War Whoop: or Indian Massacres and War in Minnesota, of 1862–3* [1863]. Edited by Dale L. Morgan. Reprinted. Chicago: R. R. Donnelley & Sons, 1965.

Neill, Rev. Edward D. *The History of Minnesota from the Earliest French Explorations to the Present Time.* Minneapolis: Minnesota Historical Company, 1883.

Pond, S. W., Jr. *Two Volunteer Missionaries among the Dakota or the Story of the Labors of Samuel W. and Gideon H. Pond.* Boston: Congregational Sunday-School and Publishing Society, 1893.

Pond, Samuel W. *The Dakota or Sioux in Minnesota as They Were in 1834.* Introduction by Gary Clayton Anderson. St. Paul: Minnesota Historical Society Press, 1986.

Renville, Mrs. Mary Butler. *A Thrilling Narrative of Indian Captivity.* Minneapolis: Atlas Company's Books and Job Office, 1863.

Report of the Commissioner of Indian Affairs for the Year 1861. Washington, D.C.: U.S. Government Printing Office, 1862.

Report of the Commissioner of Indian Affairs for the Year 1862. Washington, D.C.: U.S. Government Printing Office, 1863.

Report of the Commissioner of Indian Affairs for the Year 1863. Washington, D.C.: U.S. Government Printing Office, 1864.

Riggs, Rev. Stephen R. *Mary and I: Forty Years with the Sioux.* Chicago: W. G. Holmes, 1880.

————. *A Memorial Discourse on Rev. Thomas S. Williamson, M.D., Mission to the Dakota Indians.* New York: American Tract Society, n.d.

————. *Tah-Koo Wah-Kan, or The Gospel among the Dakotas.* Boston: Congregational Sabbath-School and Publishing Society, 1869.

Satterlee, Marion P. *A Detailed Account of the Massacre by Dakota Indians of Minnesota in 1862.* Minneapolis: Marion P. Satterlee, 1923.

Schwandt, Mary. "The Story of Mary Schwandt. Her Captivity during the Sioux 'Outbreak,'—1862." *Minnesota Historical Society Collections* 6 (1896): 461–74.

"Taoyateduta Is Not a Coward." *Minnesota History* 38 (September 1962): 115.

Upham, Warren, and Rose Barteau, comps. *Collections of the Minnesota Historical Society, Minnesota Biographies 1655–1912.* St. Paul: Dunlap, 1912.

Whipple, Henry Benjamin, D.D., LL.D. *Lights and Shadows of a Long Episcopate: Being Reminiscences and Recollections of the Right Reverend Henry Benjamin Whipple.* New York: Macmillan Company, 1899.

White, Mrs. N. D. [Urania Frazer]. "Captivity among the Sioux, August 18 to September 26, 1862." *Minnesota Historical Society Collections* 9 (April 1901): 395–426.

SECONDARY WORKS

A rich background to Wakefield's world can be gleaned from several sources. Gary Clayton Anderson, *Kinsmen of Another Kind: Dakota-White Relations in the Upper Mississippi Valley, 1650–1862* (Lincoln: University of Nebraska Press, 1984) is the best work on Native-white relations in nineteenth-century Minnesota. Roy W. Meyer's *History of the Santee Sioux: United States Indian Policy on Trial,* rev. ed. (Lincoln: University of Nebraska, 1993), follows the story of the Dakota War into the late nineteenth century. Robert M. Utley's *The Last Days of the Sioux Nation* (New Haven: Yale University Press, 1963) places the Dakota War in the larger context of Sioux history. David A. Nichols, *Lincoln and the Indians: Civil War Policy and Politics* (Columbia: University of Missouri Press, 1978), gives a sense of the political context of Indian relations in the Lincoln years. William Watts Folwell, *A History of Minnesota,* 4 vols. (St. Paul: Minnesota Historical Society Press, 1924), is an older but still a useful work on Minnesota history.

Other secondary sources include the following:

Albers, Patricia, and Beatrice Medicine. *The Hidden Half: Studies of Plains Indian Women.* Washington, D.C: University Press of America, 1983.

Anderson, Gary Clayton. *Little Crow: Spokesman for the Sioux.* St. Paul: Minnesota Historical Society Press, 1986.

Armitage, Susan, and Elizabeth Jameson, eds. *The Women's West.* Norman: University of Oklahoma Press, 1987.

Axtell, James. *The European and the Indian: Essays in the Ethnohistory of Colonial North America.* New York: Oxford University Press, 1981.

————. *The Invasion Within: The Conquest of Cultures in Colonial America.* New York: Oxford University Press, 1985.

————. *Natives and Newcomers: The Cultural Origins of North America.* New York: Oxford University Press, 2001.

Bataille, Gretchen M., and Kathleen Mullen Sands. *American Indian Women: Telling Their Lives.* Lincoln: University of Nebraska Press, 1984.

Baym, Nina. *Novels, Readers, and Reviewers: Responses to Fiction in Antebellum America.* 2d ed. Ithaca, N.Y.: Cornell University Press, 1993.

————. *Woman's Fiction: A Guide to Novels by and about Women in America, 1820–1870.* 2d ed. Urbana: Univ. of Illinois Press, 1993.

Behar, Ruth, and Deborah A. Gordon, eds. *Women Writing Culture.* Berkeley: University of California Press, 1995.

Berkhofer, Robert F., Jr. "White Conceptions of Indians." In *History of Indian-White Relations*, ed. Wilcomb E. Washburn. Vol. 4 of *Handbook of North American Indians*, ed. William C. Sturtevant. Washington D.C.: Smithsonian Institution, 1988. 522–47.

————. *The White Man's Indian: Images of the American Indian from Columbus to the Present.* New York: Vintage Books-Random House, 1979.

Billington, Ray Allen. *Land of Savagery, Land of Promise: The European Image of the American Frontier in the Nineteenth Century.* New York: W. W. Norton, 1981.

Bush, Alfred L., and Lee Clark Mitchell. *The Photograph and the American Indian.* Princeton: Princeton University Press, 1994.

Calloway, Colin G. *The American Revolution in Indian Country: Crisis and Diversity in Native American Communities.* New York: Cambridge University Press, 1995.

————, ed. *New Directions in American Indian History.* Norman: University of Oklahoma Press, 1988.

Carley, Kenneth. *The Sioux Uprising of 1862.* St. Paul: Minnesota Historical Society Press, 1976.

Castiglia, Christopher. *Bound and Determined: Captivity, Culture-Crossing, and White Womanhood from Mary Rowlandson to Patty Hearst.* Chicago: University of Chicago Press, 1996.

Clifford, James. *The Predicament of Culture.* Cambridge: Harvard University Press, 1988.

Clifford, James, and Vivek Dhareshwar, eds. *Traveling Theories, Traveling Theorists.* Inscriptions, vol. 5. Santa Cruz CA: The Center for Cultural Studies, UCSC, 1989.

DeMallie, Raymond J., and Alfonso Ortiz, eds. *North American Indian Anthropology: Essays on Society and Culture.* Norman: University of Oklahoma Press, 1994.

DeMallie, Raymond J., and Elaine A. Jahner, eds. *Lakota Belief and Ritual.* Lincoln: University of Nebraska Press, 1980.

DeMallie, Raymond J., and Douglas R. Parks, eds. *Sioux Indian Religion.* Norman: University of Oklahoma Press, 1987.

D'Emilio, John, and Estelle B. Freedman. *Intimate Matters: A History of Sexuality in America.* New York: Harper & Row, 1988.

Derounian-Stodala, Kathryn Zabelle, and James Arthur Levernier. *The Indian Captivity Narrative, 1550–1900.* New York: Twayne Publishers, 1993.

Douglas, Ann. *The Feminization of American Culture.* New York: Alfred A. Knopf, 1977.

Drinnon, Richard. *Facing West: The Metaphysics of Indian-Hating and Empire Building.* Minneapolis: University of Minnesota Press, 1980.

———. *White Savage: The Case of John Dunn Hunter.* New York: Schocken Books, 1972.

Erdoes, Richard, and Alfonso Ortiz, eds. *American Indian Myths and Legends.* New York: Pantheon, 1984.

Etienne, Mona, and Eleanor Leacock, eds. *Women and Colonization: Anthropological Perspectives.* New York: Praeger, 1980.

Ewers, John C., ed. *Plains Indian History and Culture: Essays on Continuity and Change.* Norman: University of Oklahoma Press, 1997.

Faragher, John Mack. *Women and Men on the Overland Trail.* New Haven, Conn.: Yale University Press, 1979.

Fleming, Paula Richardson, and Judith Luskey. *The North American Indians in Early Photographs.* New York: Harper & Row, 1986.

Foucault, Michel. *Discipline and Punish: The Birth of the Prison.* Trans. Alan Sheridan. New York: Vintage, 1995.

Frederickson, George M. *White Supremacy: A Comparative Study of American and South African History.* New York: Oxford University Press, 1981.

Gilligan, Carol. *Psychological Theory and Women's Development.* Cambridge, Mass.: Harvard University Press, 1982.

Ginzberg, Lori D. *Women and the Work of Benevolence: Morality, Politics, and Class in the Nineteenth-Century United States.* New Haven, Conn.: Yale University Press, 1990.

Green, Rayna. *Native American Women: A Contextual Bibliography.* 1984.

———. *Women in American Indian Society.* New York: Chelsea House, 1984.

Heard, Norman J. *White into Red: A Study of Assimilation of White Persons Captured by Indians.* Metuchen, N.J.: Scarecrow Press, 1973.

Hodes, Martha. *White Women, Black Men: Illicit Sex in the Nineteenth-Century South.* New Haven: Yale University Press, 1997.

———, ed. *Sex, Love, Race: Crossing Boundaries in North American History.* New York: New York University Press, 1999.

Horsman, Reginald. *Race and Manifest Destiny: The Origins of American Racial Anglo-Saxonism.* Cambridge, Mass.: Harvard University Press, 1981.

Hoxie, Frederick E., ed. *Indians in American History: An Introduction.* Arlington Heights IL: Harlan Davidson, 1998.

Hultkrantz, Åke. *Native Religions of North America: The Power of Visions and Fertility.* New York: Harper & Row, 1987.

———. *The Religions of the American Indians.* Translated by Monica Setterwall. Berkeley: University of California Press, 1967.

Jeffrey, Julie Roy. *Frontier Women: The Trans-Mississippi West 1840–1880.* New York: Hill and Wang, 1979.

Katz, Jane, ed. *Messengers of the Wind: Native American Women Tell Their Life Stories.* New York: Ballantine Books, 1995.

Kestler, Frances Roe, comp. *The Indian Captivity Narrative: A Woman's View.* New York: Garland Publishing, 1990.

Kittay, Eva Feder, and Diana T. Meyers, eds. *Women and Moral Theory.* Totowa, N.J.: Rowman & Littlefield, 1987.

Klein, Laura F., and Lillian A. Ackerman, eds. *Women and Power in Native North America.* Norman: University of Oklahoma Press, 1995.

Kolodny, Annette. *The Land before Her: Fantasy and Experience of the American Frontiers, 1630–1860.* Chapel Hill: University of North Carolina Press, 1984.

Kuper, Adam. *The Invention of Primitive Society: Transformations of an Illusion.* New York: Routledge,1988.

Kupperman, Karen Ordahl. *Indians and English: Facing Off in Early America.* Ithaca: Cornell University Press, 2000.

Landes, Ruth. *The Mystic Lake Sioux: Sociology of the Mdewakanton Santee.* Madison: University of Wisconsin Press, 1968.

Lass, William E. *Minnesota: A Bicentennial History.* New York: W. W. Norton, 1977.

Lowie, Robert H. *Indians of the Plains* [1954]. Reprinted. Garden City, N.Y.: American Museum of Natural History Press, 1963.

Lystra, Karen. *Searching the Heart: Women, Men, and Romantic Love in Nineteenth-Century America.* New York: Oxford University Press, 1989.

Martin, Calvin, ed. *The American Indian and the Problem of History.* New York: Oxford University Press, 1987.

———. *The Way of the Human Being.* New Haven: Yale University Press, 1999.

McPherson, James M. *Battle Cry of Freedom: The Civil War Era.* New York: Oxford University Press, 1988.

Minnesota History News 28 (November/December 1987).

Momaday, N. Scott. Introduction to *With Eagle Glance: American Indian Photographic Images, 1868 to 1931.* An Exhibition of Selected Photographs from the Collection of Warren Adelson and Ira Spanierman. New York: Museum of the North American Indian, 1982.

Namias, June. "White Captives: Gender and Ethnicity on Successive American Frontiers, 1607–1862." Ph.D. diss. Brandeis University, 1988.

———. *White Captives: Gender and Ethnicity on the American Frontier.* Chapel Hill: University of North Carolina Press, 1993.

Neihardt, John G. (as told through). *Black Elk Speaks, Being the Life Story of a Holy Man of the Oglala Sioux.* Lincoln: University of Nebraska Press, 1979.

Pearce, Roy Harvey. *Savagism and Civilization: A Study of the Indian and the American Mind.* Revised ed. Berkeley: University of California Press, 1988.

————. "The Significance of the Captivity Narrative." *American Literature* 19 (March 1947): 1–20.

Perdue, Theda. *Cherokee Women: Gender and Culture Change, 1700–1835.* Lincoln: University of Nebraska, 1998.

————, ed. *Sifters: Native American Women's Lives.* New York: Oxford University Press, 2001.

Powers, Marla N. *Oglala Women: Myth, Ritual, and Reality.* Chicago: University of Chicago Press, 1986.

Prucha, Francis Paul. *The Great Father: The United States Government and the American Indians.* Abr. ed. Lincoln: University of Nebraska Press, 1986.

Riley, Glenda. *Women and Indians on the Frontier, 1825–1915.* Albuquerque: University of New Mexico Press, 1984.

Ryan, Mary P. *Women and the Work of Benevolence: Morality, Politics, and Class in the Nineteenth-Century United States.* New Haven, Conn.: Yale University Press, 1990.

———— *Women in Public: Between Banners and Ballots, 1825–1880.* Baltimore: Johns Hopkins University Press, 1990.

Sandweiss, Martha A., ed. *Photography in Nineteenth-Century America.* Fort Worth: Amon Carter Museum; New York: Harry N. Abrams, 1991.

Scott, Joan Wallach. *Gender and the Politics of History.* New York: Columbia University Press, 1988.

Shoemaker, Nancy, ed. *Negotiators of Change: Historical Perspectives on Native American Women.* New York: Routledge, 1995.

Showalter, Elaine, ed. *Feminist Criticism: Essays on Women, Literature, and Theory.* New York: Pantheon, 1985.

Slotkin, Richard. *The Fatal Environment: The Myth of the Frontier in the Age of Industrialization, 1800–1890.* New York: Athenaeum, 1985.

————. *Regeneration through Violence: The Mythlolgy of the American Frontier, 1600–1860.* Middletown, Conn.: Wesleyan University Press, 1973.

Smith, Henry Nash. *Virgin Land: The American West as Symbol and Myth.* New York: Vintage, 1959.

Smith, Sidonie. *A Poetics of Women's Autobiography: Marginality and the Fictions of Self Representation.* Bloomington: Indiana University Press, 1987.

————. *Subjectivity, Identity, and the Body: Women's Autobiographical Practices in the Twentieth-Century.* Bloomington: Indiana University Press, 1993.

Smith, Sidonie, and Julia Watson, eds. *De/Colonizing the Subject: The Politics of Gender in Women's Autobiography.* Minneapolis: University of Minnesota Press, 1992.

Smith-Rosenberg, Carroll. *Disorderly Conduct: Visions of Gender in Victorian America.* New York: Alfred A. Knopf, 1985.

Strong, Pauline Turner. *Captive Selves, Captivating Others: The Politics and Poetics of Colonial American Captivity Narratives.* Boulder CO: Westview Press, 1999.

Stuhler, Barbara, and Gretchen Kreuter, eds. *Women of Minnesota: Selected Biographical Essays.* St. Paul: Minnesota Historical Society Press, 1977.

Tedlock, Dennis, and Barbara Tedlock, eds. *Teachings from the American Earth: Indian Religion and Philosophy.* New York: Liveright, 1975.

Tompkins, Jane P. *Sensational Designs: The Cultural Work of American Fiction, 1790–1860.* New York: Oxford University Press, 1985.

Underhill, Ruth. *Red Man's America: A History of Indians in the United States.* Revised ed. Chicago: University of Chicago Press, 1971.

Unruh, John D., Jr. *The Plains Across: The Overland Emigrants and the Trans-Mississippi West, 1840–1860.* Urbana: University of Illinois Press, 1982.

VanDerBeets, Richard. *The Indian Captivity Narrative: An American Genre.* Lanham, Md.: University Press of America, 1984.

Van Kirk, Sylvia. *Many Tender Ties: Women on Fur Trade Society, 1670–1870.* Norman: University of Oklahoma Press, 1980.

Vexler, Robert I., and William F. Swindler. *Chronology and Documentary Handbook of the State of Minnesota.* Dobbs Ferry, N.Y.: Oceana, 1978.

Wallace, Anthony F. C. *The Long, Bitter Trail: Andrew Jackson and the Indians.* New York: Hill and Wang, 1993.

Washburn, Wilcomb E. *Red Man's Land/White Man's Law: A Study of the Past and Present Status of the American Indian.* New York: Charles Scribner's Sons, 1971.

White, Richard. *The Middle Ground: Indians, Empires, and Republics in the Great Lakes Region, 1650–1815.* New York: Cambridge University Press, 1991.

Wilson, Raymond. *Ohiyesa: Charles Eastman, Santee Sioux.* Urbana: University of Illinois Press, 1983.

Wong, Hertha Dawn. *Sending My Heart Back across the Years: Tradition and Innovation in Native American Autobiography.* New York: Oxford University Press, 1992.

Yellin, Jean Fagan, *Women and Sisters: The Antislavery Feminists in American Culture.* New Haven, Conn.: Yale University Press, 1989.

Young, Mary E. "Women, Civilization, and the Indian Question." In *Women's America: Refocusing the Past,* 149–55. Edited by Linda K. Kerber and Jane De Hart Mathews. New York: Oxford University Press, 1982.

Zboray, Ronald J. *A Fictive People: Antebellum Economic Development and the American Reading Public.* New York: Oxford University Press, 1993.

INDEX